To Tim,   Aug 2010

Very Happy Birthday +
much love.

Auntie Lou.
                                    x

Trout & Salmon
FLIES of IRELAND

Trout & Salmon
FLIES of IRELAND

PETER O'REILLY

FLIES TIED BY PETER O'REILLY
AND PHOTOGRAPHED BY TERRY GRIFFITHS

MERLIN UNWIN BOOKS

First published in Great Britain by Merlin Unwin Books, 1995
Reprinted 1996, 2002 and 2004
ISBN 1 873674 19 8

Published by
Merlin Unwin Books
7 Corve Street, Ludlow, Shropshire SY8 1DB
Telephone: +44 (01584) 877456 Fax: +44 (01584) 877457
Email: books@merlinunwin.co.uk   www.countrybooksdirect.com

British Library Cataloguing-in-Publication Data:
A catalogue record for this book is available from the British
Library.

Designed and typeset in Caslon by Merlin Unwin Books.
Printed in China by Leo Paper Products.

Contents

Illustrations

To my son
Patrick
and to the next generation
of fly fishers

Acknowledgements

A ny attempts to compile a comprehensive list of fly patterns covering brown trout, seatrout and salmon in both river and lough requires a lot of research and thought. From the thousands of patterns that are used every season it is necessary to strike a balance when choosing the final list. A little knowledge may be gained by personal experience, research and discovery, but most of what we know about flies is gleaned from the experience of others. In Ireland, many of the effective fly patterns become popular and established by being talked about by anglers. They have their roots in the oral tradition and are not always written down. An angling writer must, therefore, dip into the waters of the wider angling experience and knowledge in order to draw his conclusions. My objective here is to provide a comprehensive list of the most effective patterns to suit just about every fishing situation. In the accompanying notes I have tried to provide the reader with the necessary background information to feel confident about using a particular fly. This information is derived from my own experiences on river and lough and of course those of many other anglers.

My thanks are due to a lot of people. Top of the list must come two people: Maureen Lyons, whose gift of a Kingsmill early one morning at Kilnahard jetty on the shore of Lough Sheelin 'started it all', and my former fishing partner, the late Mick Finnegan, who provided my first flytying kit.

I am indebted to Sandy Leventon, editor of *Trout and Salmon* for permission to use material submitted over the years and to all those listed below who provided information and samples of fly patterns. Some deserve a special mention for the manner of their response and for being especially helpful, co-operative, and generous with their information. I refer to: Robert Gillespie of Foxford, for tying most of the salmon shrimp flies and for his advice on how to fish them; Peter R. Brown of Dublin, for river trout patterns; Cyril Conlon of Galway for his duckflies; Billy Quail of Portadown for river dry flies; and Andrew Ryan, Clonanav Angling Centre, Co. Waterford for wet and dry river patterns.

I also wish to acknowledge the help of: John Bradley, Dr Francis Briggs, Mickey Doherty, James Fleming, Murt Folan, Ronnie Lyttle, Michael Kelly, E.J. Malone, John Meskell, Stuart McTeare, Frankie McPhillips, Peter McGinley, Hugh O'Connor, Tony O'Donnell, Christopher Pringle, James Rooney, Cathal Rush, Noel Shields, Louis Vambeck, Michael Brown, Barrie Cooke, Kevin Clayton, Arthur Drugan, Dr Paddy Gargan, Liam Gilsenan, Dr Michael Kennedy, Peter Wolstenholme, Donald McClearn, Tommy McCutcheon, John Murphy, Cyril Murry, P.J. Nally, Vinny O'Reilly, Eddie Purcell, Noel Ross, Jack Ringrose, Christy Sleator, Mike Weaver, Dr Ken Whelan.

My thanks to Terry Griffiths for the splendid photographs of the flies, to James Carney for the back cover photograph, to Miriam Carberry for the typescript and to my publisher, Merlin Unwin, for his unfailing courtesy and patience.

Finally, my very special thanks to Rose, my wife, for her encouragement and steadfast support.

Foreword

Where the wandering water gushes
From the hills above Glencar
In pools among the rushes
That scarce could bathe a star
We fish for slumbering trout
And whispering in their ears
Give them unquiet dreams

River and lake fishing for trout and salmon can be, for those who desire to commune with nature, the ultimate joy and revelation. And fishing with the fly is the great challenge, combining as it does artistry and skill with delicate and keen purpose. For those bitten with the bug it provides an opportunity for relaxation way beyond that of any other sport. To fish late into the evening on Lough Corrib, to eat heartily, to celebrate and exaggerate the catch and to arrive back in Dublin in the early hours feeling fresh enough to drive to the moon, is part and parcel of the great joy of fishing. To concentrate all one's attention on the fly to the exclusion of worldly cares is the very champagne of life and reinvigorating to the enth degree.

Peter O'Reilly follows in the tradition of the late, loved and revered Kingsmill Moore. Like KM, he shares with us his great store of knowledge and experience, gathered over many years of fishing the multitudinous lakes and rivers of Ireland. His two previous books - one on the lakes, and the other on the rivers of Ireland - are the definite reference books of the 1990s and they excite a great expectation for this new work on flies. Knowing Peter, with his keen eye and thorough approach, I know you won't be disappointed by his latest offering.

For anglers of greater or lesser experience and knowledge, this book will place your angling on a higher plane, and it will enable you to gain ever more joy from your sport, in the beautiful surroundings of the waterside.

> Leaning softly out
> From ferns that drop their tears
> Over the young streams
> Come away o human child
> To the waters and the wild

Donal Fingleton
Chief Executive
Volkswagen Audi - Ireland

Introduction

I have never met a master of all the methods of game fishing who did not prefer to fish a fly whenever possible. Fishing the fly with skill and confidence is surely the ultimate aspiration of all anglers.

The purpose of this book is to provide a selection of tried and tested patterns for those who flyfish in Ireland for brown trout, seatrout or salmon in rivers and loughs. I hope that it will be especially useful to young and aspiring flyfishers. The illustrations will help in the recognition of fly patterns - something beginners often ask me for. They will also help flytyers to determine fly proportions and the style of particular dressings. My wish is to share with my fellow anglers many of the wonderfully effective patterns that others have shared with me, or that I have been fortunate enough to discover.

Since I first developed an interest in flytying, many years ago, I have experimented with many new patterns. Most of these I came across in books or magazine articles, gleaned from fellow anglers. I would not claim to have invented any magic flies, but over the years I have had the opportunity to gain extensive knowledge of a wide range of well-tested patterns and when, where and how to fish them. We all get to know of thousands of different patterns and try many of them. The numerous fly boxes some of us possess are testimony to this. But a line has to be drawn somewhere and what I have tried to do is present a selection of popular and well proven patterns gleaned from a variety of sources over the length and breadth of the country. Some are ancient patterns that have been tested and found useful again and again. Others are less known, have never been written up, and only get passed on by word of mouth from angler to angler on lough, shore and river bank. A few could even be described as closely guarded secrets, now willingly shared.

Not all the patterns listed are of Irish origin. This is not a book of Irish flies but rather a book of flies for Ireland. Visiting anglers have introduced many flies which have proved to be reliable takers of Irish fish and these flies have been adopted. International angling magazines are a source of new and effective dressings, which are then tied and tried, and some continue to be used because they have been found to be effective in Ireland.

To me, fly patterns fall naturally into three divisions: dry flies, wet flies and salmon flies, and that is how this book has been arranged. However, some flies would be equally happy in any section. The Green Peter, for example, can be fished either wet or dry, for trout or for salmon. And, while many would consider a Daddy to be essentially a dry fly, it was of course an Irishman who first thought of pulling it through the water as a wet fly.

I myself have tied the majority of the flies shown in the illustrations. I hope they will make the dressings easy to follow. With a few exceptions, the materials are listed in the order in which they are tied on the hook. In this way other flytyers, especially those who are in the process of learning the craft should find it a relatively simple matter to produce.

Of course it is never possible to include all the patterns that one would like, nor indeed does any one angler need all the flies that are described here, but at least I am happy that I have put together a selection of flies for Irish waters to suit nearly every situation.

Peter O'Reilly
Easter 1995

The Wet Flies

━━━━━

It is probably true to say that wet fly fishing is the most widely practised form of fishing for game fish in Ireland. Beginners nearly always start with a wet fly and some continue to use this method virtually all the time. Part of the attraction has to be the ease with which wet flies can be fished - and of course they catch an awful lot of fish. This section also includes nymphs and pupae for the reason that they often end up in the same box and are fished in similar situations or sometimes at the same time as the wet fly. I think it is the wet fly's versatility that makes it so popular. It can be used on either river or lough and will take all species equally well. Once one gets to know them well it is quite possible to find a fly in this section to cover any eventuality for brown trout, seatrout or even salmon. For example, the Green Peter, Bibio, Claret Bumble and Watson's Fancy, to name but a few, all fall into this category.

Hence it is quite possible to be well equipped for a whole range of fishing with only a small selection of flies. Of course, anglers will always want to have the widest possible choice of flies, and so we all have boxes of them, but, strictly speaking, it is possible to be quite well equipped for most eventualities with just a handful of patterns in a range of sizes. Situations arise and fishing conditions sometimes demand specific patterns but one can have a lot of fun and catch a lot of fish with a few well tied suggestive patterns, properly presented.

This section is made up of attractors and imitative patterns. It might be considered that some of the patterns in this section would be more appropriately located under 'dry flies'. That, strictly speaking, may be correct, but in Ireland anglers have a habit of fishing their dry flies wet. This is especially true of sedge patterns, and who but an Irishman would think of tying a Daddy on the point of a three-fly leader and pulling it through the water. Strange, but it works!

Alexandra

PLATE 1

Hook: Size 8-12 Partridge L2A
Tying silk: Black
Tail: Red ibis substitute or slip of swan, dyed scarlet
Body: Flat silver tinsel
Rib: Oval silver tinsel
Hackle: Black cock or hen hackle
Wing: A pinch of green peacock sword fibres with slips of red ibis substitute or scarlet swan tied on either side

This is primarily a lough pattern. It is mainly used for brown trout in summer when the perch fry are about. It is usually fished on the point and a size 10 is the most popular.

In Connemara it is frequently used as a seatrout fly on both river and lough. Here, the red ibis substitute on the wing is often replaced with jungle cock and this variant is known as the Jungle Alexandra.

Amber Nymph

PLATE 1

Hook: Size 10 or 12 Partridge JIA
Tying silk: Golden olive or primrose.
Wing case: A slip of any brown feather, e.g. dark turkey tail, tied in well round the bend of the hook and tied off behind the thorax
Rib: Oval gold tinsel
Body: Amber seal's fur tied quite thick. A good alternative shade is obtained by mixing one part of golden olive seal's fur and two parts of lemon yellow
Thorax: Brown seal's fur
Throat: A pinch of golden olive or honey hackle fibres tied as a beard hackle

This is an English pattern from the 1920s. The 'nymph' name is misleading, as it is really a sedge pupa imitation. I first saw it used to good effect on Lough Sheelin by Arthur Cove, though his dressing substituted rabbit fur for the brown seal's fur of the thorax. It is usually fished on the point with a slow retrieve and may be allowed to sink well. The body should be tied quite thick and make sure it starts round the bend of the hook.

Apple Green Pupa

PLATE 1

Hook: Size 12 Partridge EIA
Tying silk: Primrose or black
Rib: Black tying silk
Body: Gütermann's sewing cotton, shade 616
Thorax: Hare's body fur or pale hare's ear tied small and neat
Hackle: One and a half turns of short badger hen. The hackle should be tied sparse

The apple-green midge (*Endochironomus albipennis*) hatches during the day and early evening between June and August. It is easily recognised by its bright apple-green or insect-green body and pale white wings. If there is a big hatch of this fly trout will feed avidly on it. In fact it is rare to spoon a trout during the summer months on the limestone loughs and not find at least some apple-green pupae in it. This pattern was first tried by Peter McGinley of Kells. I have absolute confidence in it and have some great memories of good trout taken on it on both Sheelin and Ennell. Fish it on a fine leader in the path of a feeding trout and do not retrieve.

Badger & Black

PLATE 1

Hook: Size 12-16 Partridge L2A
Tying silk: Black
Tail: Badger cock hackle fibres

PLATE 1: WET FLIES

Top Row Ballinderry Black, Alexandra, Black & Orange
1st Row Amber Nymph, Bibio, Bibio Variant, Apple Green Pupa
2nd Row Baby Doll, Badger & Black, Baltic Special
3rd Row Black Buzzer Nymph, Black Chironomid Pupa
4th Row Black & Peacock Spider, Black Sedge, Black Pennell
Bottom Row Black Widow, Blae & Black, Blae Sooty Olive

Body: Black silk
Hackle: Badger hen or cock

This is a river pattern, and is best fished on the dropper. It is probably taken by the trout for a small black midge that has been caught on the surface and is being swept downstream.

Baby Doll (Brian Kench)

PLATE 1

Hook: Size 6-10 Kamasan B170
Tying silk: Black
Body: White nylon wool or fluorescent white wool
Tail: Body wool well picked out
Back: Two strands of body wool
Head: Black silk, well built up and varnished

The Baby Doll was first tied by the Englishman Brian Kench in 1971. It can be an excellent lure and most effective, in my experience, when the trout are on the perch fry in late June and July. But it can produce a trout at any time and is a good fallback in water with an algal bloom and poor visibility. Fish it on either a floating or a sinking line. When trout are attacking fry and the tiny fish are dimpling the surface like rain drops in their efforts to escape, cast a greased Baby Doll among the fry and fish it static. When tying the pattern, take a 12-inch length of wool. Double it twice and tie it in on top at the end of the hook, leaving half an inch extending for the tail. Then wrap two strands around the shank to form the body and take the other two over the top and tie off at the head.

Ballinderry Black

PLATE 1

Hook: Size 8-12 Partridge AIA
Tying silk: Black

Tag: Golden yellow floss silk
Rib: Flat gold tinsel
Tail: Golden pheasant tippet
Body: Black seal's fur
Hackle: Black hen or cock
Wing: Bronze mallard with a golden pheasant tippet insert.

This is one of Tommy Hanna's creations from Northern Ireland. It is popular as a lough fly, fished on the dropper, and it is also a good taker of dollaghan trout in the Lough Neagh rivers.

Baltic Special

PLATE 1

Hook: Size 8 longshank, silver-plated
Tying silk: Red
Body: Pearl Lureflash
Wing: Pearl Lureflash with blue Lureflash tied over
Head: Red

This is the pattern with which I cracked the secret of how to catch seatrout on fly on the Moy estuary in 1994. Its origins are in northern Germany on the Baltic Sea. It was given to P.J. Nally of Castlebar by Hans Eiber, a German angling writer. Fish it with a fast retrieve on a fine leader and intermediate line. When the shoals of seatrout are located, it is immediately grabbed by the trout and gets a reaction on almost every cast. Fish only two flies on the leader with this one on the point.

Bibio (Charles Roberts)

PLATE 1

Hook: Size 8-14 Partridge L2A
Tying silk: Black
Rib: Fine oval silver wire
Body: Seal's fur in three parts - black, hot orange and black

Hackle: Black cock palmered, with a second black cock hackle, slightly longer in the fibre, at the front

A fly created in the late fifties or early sixties by Major Charles Roberts, of the Burrishoole Fishery in Mayo. It was originally tied to represent the heather beetle for seatrout on loughs Furnace and Feeagh. However, it has become one of the really great Irish wet flies for brown trout, seatrout and salmon. It can be fished on the lough in any position on the leader and is taken for a wide range of dark insects from duckflies to beetles. The water conditions usually determine the size to be fished. It is also a very good taker of salmon and seatrout when fished on the dropper on rippled pools in West of Ireland rivers.

Some anglers consider that a black hen hackle tied in front, instead of the cock hackle, improves the effectiveness of this fly, giving it a more waterlogged apearance as a bob fly.

Bibio Variant

PLATE 1

Hook: Size 8-12
Tying silk: Black
Rib: Two strands of fine pearl Lureflash
Body: Seal's fur in three parts - black, hot orange and black
Hackle: Black cock palmered with a brown partridge hackle at the head

How do you improve on perfection? The Bibio is a great fly in its own right. This variation originated, to the best of my knowledge, at Lough Corrib and has proved to be a superb fly in a big wave and a valuable addition to any fly box. It began life as a brown trout lough fly for late summer, but I am quite sure it has wider uses. Particularly good for rainbow trout.

Black Buzzer Nymph

PLATE 1

Hook: Size 12-16 Kamasan B175
Tying silk: Black
Rib: Fine silver Mylar
Body: Black seal's fur dressed around the bend of the hook
Thorax: Bronze peacock herl
Hackle: Short black hen

This fly combines the best features of Arthur Cove's Black Pupa and Peter Brown's Black Buzzer which, between them, have taken thousands of trout. This pattern can be used either when buzzers are hatching on the lough or dark midges are about on the river.

Black Chironomid Pupa

PLATE 1

Hook: Size 12-16 Kamasan B170
Tying silk: Black
Rib: Fine copper wire
Tail: A few fibres of white hackle tied short
Body: Strip of crow wing quill tied well around the bend of the hook
Wing case: Crow wing fibres
Thorax: As for the body, and kept small
Breathers: Small tuft of white wool

I first tied this pattern for chironomid-feeding trout on Lough Sheelin in the early seventies. I found it worked well when cast to trout taking pupae in the surface film and fished stationary or retrieved very slowly. It appears to fish best when dressed on a light-wire, sproat-bend hook.

Black & Orange

PLATE 1

Hook: Size 10-12 Partridge JIA
Tying silk: Orange
Rib: Fine oval gold tinsel

Tail: Golden pheasant tippet
Body: Orange floss
Hackle: Black hen or cock
Wing: Strips of crow wing

This is an old pattern. It is usually fished on the bob at duckfly time, but it can also be effective as a point fly on the loughs early in the season.

Black & Peacock Spider

PLATE 1

Hook: Size 10-12 Partridge JIA
Tying silk: Black
Body: Bronze peacock herl built up
Hackle: Black hen, three turns

It is sometimes said that there is nothing new in fishing. The Black & Peacock Spider was popularised by England's Tom Ivens in the 1960s. I have recently discovered that the same fly, then known as the Black Hackle, was listed as a seatrout fly for the River Lagan in the handbook of artificial flies prepared for the Department of Agriculture's fishery exhibit at the Cork Exhibition in 1902. Today, the Black & Peacock is regarded as a lough fly for both brown trout and seatrout. It can be particularly effective on a size 12 hook in the month of August when snails are migrating. Fish it slowly and close to the surface. I have also found it to be an effective bob fly on the lough fished in a wave at dusk close to the shore.

Black Pennell

PLATE 1

Hook: Size 8-14 Partridge L2A
Tying silk: Black
Tag: Fine oval silver
Rib: Fine oval silver
Tail: Golden pheasant tippet

Body: Black floss silk
Hackle: Black hen or cock, long in fibre

Hackled wet flies are commonly used on Irish loughs. The Black Pennell is one such fly. It takes brown trout, seatrout and salmon equally well. I prefer to fish it on the bob for salmon and it once had a great reputation as a taker of salmon at Burrishoole. I think it is more effective fished on the point for brown trout and especially for seatrout. It is a particularly good fly for seatrout during the day when tied with a sparse hackle and dressed on a size 12 or 14 hook and fished on a fine leader. It is often tied without the tag.

Black Sedge

PLATE 1

Hook: Size 12 Kamasan B175
Tying silk: Black
Rib: Gold wire
Body: Black seal's fur
Wings: Crow secondary tied low to body
Hackle: Dark Greenwell or dark red-brown hackle

A dressing to imitate the Welshman's Button, also called the Dark Caperer. The natural hatches during the day and early evening in late May and June and is fairly widely distributed. It is found mainly on fast-flowing rivers and this pattern can be fished wet on the dropper in fast runs, especially in the evening.

The Welshman's Button also hatches on some of the loughs, such as Lough Ennell.

Black Widow

PLATE 1

Hook: Size 6-12 Partridge L2A
Tying silk: Black
Rib: Fine oval silver

PLATE 2: WET FLIES

Top Row Bloody Butcher, Blood Worm (McTeare), Blue & Black
1st Row Blue Dun, Bluebottle, Blue-Winged Olive
2nd Row Blue Zulu, BWO Emerger, BWO Nymph, Bog Fly
3rd Row Brigg's Pennell, Butcher, Bruiser
4th Row Campto Emerger, Camasunary Killer, Cinnamon & Gold
Bottom Row Claret Bumble, Claret Chironomid Pupa, Claret Dabbler

Tail: Golden pheasant topping
Body: Black Floss
Hackle: Furnace cock or hen
Wing: Bronze mallard

I have only ever seen this pattern fished for seatrout at night at Ballynahinch where it was quite successful. It is often fished in quite large sizes, such as a longshank size 8 or even a 6.

Blae & Black

PLATE 1

Hook: Size 10-14 Partridge L2A
Tying silk: Black
Rib: Fine oval silver tinsel
Body: Black floss
Hackle: Black hen
Wing: Starling.

This is a well tried and trusted pattern, especially on the loughs when Duckfly are hatching early in the season. It gives good results when fished on the bob in small sizes (12 or 14), but it is at its best when fished on a slow-sinking line in a ripple in areas where fly are hatching. It is amazing how it will take trout after trout, even when no fish are showing.

Blae Sooty Olive
(Vincent O'Reilly)

PLATE 1

Hook: Size 10-14 Partridge JIA
Tying silk: Black
Rib: Fine oval silver tinsel
Tail: Golden pheasant tippets
Body: Sooty olive seal's fur (dark olive and brown olive mixed in equal parts)
Hackle: Sooty olive cock
Wing: Slips of jay primary

The Blae Sooty is a pattern I first saw tied by

Vincent O'Reilly of Headford on Lough Corrib. It is a very popular top dropper fly on the western loughs in March and April when duckfly are hatching, and later on for olive buzzers and lake olives. It seems to be at its best when fished lough-style as one of a team of three or four flies. The size is determined by water conditions - size 10 in a good wave and size 12 in a small wave or ripple. Trout will take this fly, fished static in a ripple, during the evening rise to the duckfly.

Blood Worm (S. McTeare)

PLATE 2

Hook: Size 8 Kamasan B170
Tying silk: Golden olive or primrose
Rib: Flat silver tinsel
Body: Rear two-thirds, red seal's fur, front third, pale olive seal's fur. The body should be dressed well round the bend of the hook.

The blood-worm is the larva of the larger chironomids. It normally lives in the mud at the bottom of a lough. Some are deep crimson in colour and others pale olive. They can measure up to 17-20mm long. Several times in Lough Sheelin in July and early August trout can be seen rising but there are no fly about. It is only when a trout is caught and its stomach contents examined that the riddle is solved. They are feeding on blood-worms floating under the surface film. Stuart McTeare, who has an angling centre at Sheelin, devised this pattern and it is so effective, fished on a floating line, that I would use no other.

Bloody Butcher

PLATE 2

Hook: Size 8-12 Partridge L2A
Tying silk: Black
Rib: Fine oval silver

Tail: Red ibis substitute or red swan
Body: Flat silver tinsel
Hackle: Scarlet or red (dyed) cock
Wing: Slip of blue mallard wing feather

I regard the Bloody Butcher as primarily an evening and night seatrout fly and in that role it is one of my top six best flies. I have had great success with it at Ballynahinch, Lough Inagh and the Gowla Fishery. On the lough I fish it on the middle dropper on a three-fly cast and on the river at night it goes on the point, of a two-fly cast. A size 10 gives best results at night.

Blue & Black

PLATE 2

Hook: Size 12-14 Partridge JIA
Tying silk : Black
Rib: Flat silver tinsel
Body: Dark blue floss
Hackle: Black hen
Wing: Starling

A very old Irish pattern from the last century, it is still used by some anglers even today for river fishing. It is more popular in the smaller sizes and is probably fished as an attractor for both browns and seatrout.

Bluebottle (wet)

PLATE 2

Hook: Size 8-10 Partridge L2A
Tying silk: Black
Tag: Oval silver tinsel
Body: Deep gentian blue chenille or kingfisher blue chenille.
Hackle: Natural black hen.

A traditional seatrout pattern, very popular in the West of Ireland, especially on Lough Beltra.

Old hands claim that the shade of blue is important and they abhor a pale blue body.

Sizes 8 and 10 are the most popular sizes.

Blue Dun

PLATE 2

Hook: Size 12-14 Partridge JIA
Tying silk: Black
Tail: Fibres of blue dun cockle hackle
Body: Blue rabbit underfur
Hackle: Blue dun cock
Wing: Starling

A good general-purpose pattern for rivers. It can be fished at any time when olives are about or can be fished 'on the blind' in streamy water.

Blue-Winged Olive Nymph

PLATE 2

Hook: Size 14
Tying silk: Brown
Rib: Fine gold wire
Tail: Fibres of bronze mallard
Body: Rust-coloured fine dubbing.
Wing case: Strip of dark brown feather
Thorax: As body
Throat hackle: Brown partridge.

This is a pattern for rivers and is best fished on a dead drift when blue-winged olives are hatching in the summer and early autumn.

Blue-Winged Olive Emerger

PLATE 2

Hook: Size 14, Kamasan B170
Tying silk: Orange
Rib: Fine gold wire
Tail: Fibres of bronze mallard
Body: Rust-coloured fine dubbing.
Hackle: Blue dun tied parachute-style

It is difficult to say whether this is a wet fly or dry fly. It is best when fished damp right in the surface film. Fish it upstream or across and allow it to drift without drag when trout are taking BWOs at the surface.

Blue-Winged Olive (wet)

PLATE 2

Hook: Size 14 or 16 Partridge JIA
Tying silk: Black
Tail: Fibres of blue dun cock hackle
Body: Stripped peacock eye quill
Hackle: Medium olive
Wing: Slips of jay primary, tied with the chalky sides in

A useful pattern for the river when BWOs are hatching.

Blue Zulu

PLATE 2

Hook: Size 8-12 Partridge L2A
Tying silk: Black
Rib: Fine oval silver tinsel
Body: Black seal's fur
Hackle: Black cock palmered with bright blue (teal blue or kingfisher blue) hackle wound in front

Chiefly regarded as a seatrout fly. It is at its best as a bob fly when the trout are fresh in the lough. It is also a useful pattern for fresh grilse on the river, especially on deep pools of west coast rivers.

Bog Fly

PLATE 2

Hook: Size 10-14 Partridge JIA
Tying silk: Black
Rib: Fine oval silver
Body: Two strands of black ostrich herl wound together
Hackle: Scarlet cock

Wing: Slips of crow with slips of red swan set inside the crow

A pattern that first came to my attention on Lough Currane. It is primarily regarded as a seatrout fly but it is equally good for brown trout on mountain loughs. It probably represents a beetle that gets blown on to the water off the heather in late July, August and September. In the smaller size 14, it can be a great taker of brown trout after a spate on moorland rivers in the month of September.

Bruiser

PLATE 2

Hook: Size 8-12 Partridge L2A
Tying silk: Black
Rib: Fine oval silver tinsel
Tail: Flax blue wool
Body: Gentian blue wool
Hackle: A Gentian blue hackle and a natural black cock hackle palmered together up the body

This is one of Kingsmill Moores renowned seatrout patterns. It is considered especially effective on dull cloudy days and is still a great favourite at the Costello Fishery.

Butcher

PLATE 2

Hook: Size 8-12 Partridge L2A
Tying silk: Black
Rib: Fine oval silver
Tail: Red ibis substitute or red swan
Body: Flat silver tinsel
Hackle: Black cock
Wing: Slips of blue mallard wing feather

An old traditional pattern, still widely used today. It is equally effective on river or lough for seatrout and brown trout. It is an excellent choice for the middle dropper for

PLATE 3: WET FLIES

Top Row Claret & Jay, Claret Fly (Rush), Coachman *1st Row* Coch-y-Bondhu, Cock Robin, Connemara Black, Corixa
2nd Row Daddy Longlegs, Daddy Longlegs (Rush) *3rd Row* Dabbler, Cove's Pheasant Tail Nymph
4th Row Damsel Fly Nymph, Dark Partridge & Orange, Dark Olive (Rush)
Bottom Row Devil, Donegal Blue, Delphi Silver

fresh-run seatrout in a lough. It can be used on the river for seatrout at night. It is an excellent choice for brown trout on mountain loughs, where it may well be taken for a corixa, and there are some who recommend it highly, tied on a size 12 hook and fished on the bob, during a hatch of lake olives.

Camasunary Killer

PLATE 2

Hook: Size 8-12 Partridge L2A
Tying silk: Black
Rib: Oval silver
Tail: Royal blue wool
Body: Royal blue wool and red DFM (fluorescent) wool in two halves with the red to the front
Hackle: Black cock, long in fibre

A fly of Scottish origin that works equally well in Ireland for both salmon and seatrout. It is as a seatrout pattern that it is most effective. It works very well in the peaty water of the Connemara fisheries, especially after a rise in water, and I have had success with it as an estuary seatrout fly. It can be fished on the bob or on the point. While royal blue wool is the original dressing, I and others have found the paler shade of Cambridge blue wool to be equally effective.

Campto Emerger

PLATE 2

Hook: Size 12 Partridge JIA or Kamasan B170
Tying silk: Black
Tail: Copydex rolled on glass with segments marked with an orange pen
Body: Peacock quill stripped of herl
Wing: Starling
Hackle: A Greenwell and a badger cock hackle wound together

Head: A small pinch of green-olive and fluorescent green wool mixed, dubbed on silk and wound on tight

In the early 1980s, big numbers of campto chironomids hatched on Lough Sheelin before dusk in July and early August. These were quite large buzzers distinguished by their vertically striped black and yellow heads. They brought on great rises of trout which anglers at the time found it difficult to come to terms with. I tied the emerging campto to represent the transition from pupa to adult. It gave good results and can be fished static, at the surface, or on the middle dropper as one of a team of wet flies.

Cinnamon & Gold

PLATE 00

Hook: Size 10-12 Partridge L2A
Tying silk: Black
Rib: Fine oval gold tinsel
Tail: Golden pheasant tippets
Body: Flat gold tinsel
Hackle: Red game or ginger cock
Wing: Slips of natural cinnamon wing quill

A pattern used mainly on the loughs and probably taken by trout for a sedge. Anyway, its effectiveness is much underrated. This is a good fly for the middle dropper on summer evenings. It is equally effective if tied without a tail, which is how I prefer it.

Claret Bumble

PLATE 2

Hook: Size 8-14 Partridge L2A
Tying silk: Black
Rib: Fine oval gold
Tail: Golden pheasant tippets
Body: Claret seal's fur
Hackle: A black and a claret cock palmered together down the body

Front hackle: Blue jay

This one of Kingsmill Moores great bumble patterns and is still widely used today. It can be fished all season as a brown trout fly on the loughs and usually from June onwards for seatrout. The shade of claret for the body and hackle can vary from medium to dark and the darker shade is preferred by some on dull days at the Costello Fishery, which this fly was first tied for. It is also extremely popular as a bob fly for brown trout and is probably taken for a sedge.

When tying, leave lots of room at the head to facilitate tying in the blue jay. Strip off the dull side of the feather and tie in by the point up against the body. Then wind on four turns forward and tie off. A short guinea-fowl hackle, dyed blue, may be used as a substitute for the blue jay.

Claret Dabbler

PLATE 2

Hook: Size 10 Kamasan B830 or Size 8 Partridge L2A
Tying silk: Brown
Rib: Fine oval gold tinsel
Tail: Ten or twelve cock pheasant with tail fibres tied in equal to the length of the hook shank
Body: Claret floss silk or claret seal's fur
Hackle: A ginger cock palmered with a light claret cock hackle (three turns) at the shoulder
Wing: Slips of good-quality bronze mallard tied in all round to envelop the whole body and reaching almost to the point of the tail

A variation on Donald McClarn's original Dabbler, the Claret Dabbler has become probably even more popular than the original. It is usually fished and stripped fast on an intermediate or sinking line.

The Claret Dabbler can be fished in any position on the leader - some anglers fish

three at a time. It is particularly effective in a big wave. Trout will chase it and take it on the dibble before final lift off. The Dabbler is a favourite with competition fishers and one that is likely to be with us for some time.

Claret Fly (Cathal Rush)

PLATE 3

Hook: Size 10-12 Kamasan B160
Tying silk: Black
Rib: Broad flat silver tinsel with silver wire over it
Tail: Green Glo-Brite floss
Body: Claret seal's fur, well picked out
Hackle: Dark grouse

This is an extremely useful little fly for the loughs from May right through to the end of the season. It provokes savage takes and can be just the fly to take a bag of trout when they are really in the mood.

Claret Chironomid Pupa

PLATE 2

Hook: Size 12 Kamasan B170
Tying silk: Black
Rib: Silver wire
Tail: White cock hackle fibres tied short
Body: Claret seal's fur
Wing case: Cock pheasant tail fibres
Thorax: Bronze peacock herl
Hackle: Black hen - sparse

A pattern I tied many years ago to be fished nymph-style, close to the surface, when buzzers are hatching. To get the hackle to sit correctly, wind it in front of the thorax, then divide it and bring the wing case over the top and tie off.

Coachman

PLATE 3

Hook: Size 10-14 Partridge L2A
Tying silk: Black
Body: Bronze peacock herl
Hackle: Red game
Wing: Slips of white duck or swan

A useful pattern when fished in a wave for the evening duckfly hatch or during any hatch of large chironomids. It is also a good fly for rivers fished late at night in streamy water.

Claret & Jay

PLATE 3

Hook: Size 10-12 Partridge L2A
Tying silk: Black
Rib: Oval gold
Tail: Golden pheasant tippets
Body: Claret seal's fur
Hackle: Medium claret cock with blue jay tied in front
Wing: Bronze mallard

This is a trout version of the salmon fly of the same name. It is primarily a seatrout pattern for the loughs and is a really good point fly.

Coch-y-Bondhu

PLATE 3

Hook: Size 12-14 Partridge L2A
Tying silk: Black
Tag: Flat gold tinsel
Body: Bronze peacock herl tied thick
Hackle: Furnace cock (natural red with black centre and black tips)

This is a useful wet fly pattern for both rivers and loughs where trout are suspected of feeding on beetles. I have found beetles in trout stomachs from as early as mid-May. The effectiveness of this fly is greatly enhanced for Lough Mask by tying in a short wing consisting of a pinch of hot orange hackle fibres.

Cock Robin

PLATE 3

Hook: Size 10-14 Partridge L21
Tying silk: Black
Rib: Oval gold tinsel
Tail: Small pinch of bronze mallard fibres
Body: In two halves: golden olive seal's fur at the rear and red seal's fur at the front
Hackle: Red game
Wing: Bronze mallard

A traditional pattern for loughs, the Cock Robin will also take trout on the river, especially after a rise in water late in the season. It is regarded as a good fly on the point or in the middle when lake olives are hatching. Some like to dress the front half of the body with medium claret seal's fur. I suspect this may be more effective when buzzers of this colour are hatching.

Connemara Black

PLATE 3

Hook: Size 8-14 Partridge L2A
Tying silk: Black
Tag: Orange floss
Rib: Fine oval silver tinsel
Tail: Golden pheasant topping
Body: Black seal's fur
Hackle: Black cock or hen with blue jay tied at the throat
Wing: Bronze mallard

A most useful pattern which will take brown trout, seatrout and salmon equally well. Fish it on the middle dropper early in the season and when black buzzers are hatching. Fish a

PLATE 4: WET FLIES

Top Row Duckfly, Duckfly (hairwing), Duckfly Emerger, Duckfly Emerger Variant *1st Row* Dunkeld,
Dunkeld Nymph, Dyson *2nd Row* Extractor, Extractor (Rush), Fenian *3rd Row* Fiery Brown,
French Partridge Mayfly, Fiery Brown Bumble *4th Row* Fiery Brown Sedge, Fanwing Mayfly, Fiery Brown Spider
Bottom Row Freshwater Louse, Flourescent Green Dabbler, Freshwater Shrimp

small one on the bob if black gnat are about. It is an excellent seatrout fly fished on the point on the lough by day and or late at night on the river. For salmon try it in sizes 10 and, 12 especially on deep pools of spate rivers. Some consider that two small jungle cock eyes enhance it when black buzzers are hatching. This form has also caught seatrout on Lough Currane.

Corixa

PLATE 3

Hook: Size 12 Partridge JIA
Tying silk: Black
Tag: Flat silver tinsel
Rib: Silver wire
Body: Cream or off-white floss silk
Back: Cock pheasant centre tail fibres
Hackle: Small pinch of creamy badger hen tied in at the throat

The corixa, or lesser water boatman, is found along the margins of many lakes, especially where there is a sandy bottom. I have found it most active (and in trouts' stomachs) in August and September. Its best-known characteristic is its need to travel to the surface at intervals for a bubble of air. Trout feed on it and can generally be taken on traditional patterns such as a Zulu or a Butcher, but, for those who wish to fish a more imitative pattern, the above dressing will take trout.

Cove's Pheasant Tail Nymph

PLATE 3

Hook: Size 8-10 Partridge L2A
Tying silk: Black
Rib: Copper wire
Body: Cock pheasant centre tail fibres tied well round the bend.
Wing case: The end of the cock pheasant tail fibres used for the body

Thorax: Blue rabbit underfur

The nymph by which the great English Midlands angler Arthur Cove will always be remembered. It is more a giant buzzer pupa imitation than a nymph and makes an excellent point fly for brown trout. It probably creates an illusion for the trout of several different food items. Its slim profile means that it will sink quickly and I have taken trout on it on many of the big loughs. Fish either nymph-style or more often as a point fly on a wet-fly cast.

Dabbler (Donald McClarn)

PLATE 3

Hook: Size 8-12 Kamasan B175
Tying silk: Brown
Rib: Fine oval gold tinsel
Tail: 8-10 cock pheasant centre tail fibres
Body: Golden olive seal's fur or substitute
Hackle: Red game cock palmered with another red game hackle wound in front of the body
Wing: Bronze mallard tied in on the top and sides only - like a cloak, the originator suggests

The Dabbler is one of the great Irish wet fly patterns of recent times and has several useful variants as well. It was invented by accident when Donald McClarn of Co. Down phoned a friend for the dressing of the Gosling. This fly took the trout angling competition scene by storm in the early 1990s and was the cornerstone of the success of the great Dromore trout-fishing teams. It is without doubt a great killing pattern when stripped fast and then dibbled, on an intermediate, sinking or floating line in a good wave. It, and its variants, have accounted for numerous big wild lough brown trout, many into double figures.

Daddy Longlegs (cranefly)

PLATE 3

Hook: Size 8-10 Partridge L2A
Tying silk: Black
Rib: Fine oval gold tinsel
Body: Natural raffia, moistened
Legs: Six cock pheasant centre tail fibres, knotted once
Wing: Badger cock hackle points
Hackle: Good quality red game

A marvellous pattern and one that should be in every brown trout, seatrout and salmon angler's fly box in the month of August. Of course it is at its best when daddyies are about and being blown on to the water, but it will also work well in August/September even when they are not in evidence. I have had great success with it as a bob fly for seatrout at Delphi, but I prefer to fish it on the point for salmon (for example at Burrishoole) or for brown trout, especially on Lough Corrib. It will often get a response at that time of season when no other fly is working. I like to tie in the legs three on top of the hook and three underneath, pointing backwards. The wings are, I believe, cosmetic, and unnecessary and I have caught lots of fish on wingless versions.

Daddy Longlegs
(Cathal Rush)

PLATE 3

Hook: Size 8 Kamasan B160
Tying silk: Brown
Body: Copydex stained with a brown waterproof felt pen and then rolled
Legs: Eight pairs of cock pheasant centre tail fibres knotted two at a time with the points snipped off
Hackle: A brown and a ginger cock hackle

A pattern that can be fished wet or dry on the loughs from June to the end of the season.

Damselfly Nymph
(C. Kendall)

PLATE 3

Hook: Size 8-10 Kamasan B830
Tying silk: Green olive
Rib: Fine gold wire
Tail: Three olive cock hackle points, splayed
Abdomen: Green-olive seal's fur
Thorax cover: Any olive-dyed feather fibres tied over the thorax
Thorax: As for the abdomen, dubbed in front of the rear pair of legs and both sides of the front legs and around the eyes
Legs: Olive-dyed mallard grey flank
Eyes: 20lb BS brown monofilament with melted ends.

Brown trout feed on damselfly nymphs from very early in the season. I have seen them on their own in trout stomachs in March. It is well worth fishing this nymph on the point in fairly shallow water in loughs where damselflies are known to hatch.

Dark Olive (Cathal Rush)

PLATE 3

Hook: Size 10-12 Partridge G3A
Tying silk: Brown
Rib: Copper wire
Tail: Golden pheasant tippets dyed hot orange with a short length of orange Globrite floss over
Body: Dark olive seal's fur
Wing: Bronze mallard
Hackle: Dark red-brown cock tied as a full collar

This is mainly an early-season fly. It is effective through April to the end of the mayfly season.

Dark Partridge & Orange (Peter Brown)

PLATE 3

Hook: Size 12-16 Kamasan B170 or B175
Tying silk: Orange
Tail: Golden pheasant tippets (size 12 only)
Body: Orange floss or tying silk
Rib: Fine flat gold tinsel - none on size 16
Hackle: Brown partridge.

A fly that can be used on the dropper on either river or lough right through the season. The partridge hackle gives nice movement and trout will take it for an emerging olive or buzzer.

Delphi Silver

PLATE 3

Hook: Size 8-12 Partridge L2A
Tying silk: Black
Rib: Fine oval silver tinsel
Tail: Two small jungle cock eyes tied back to back
Body: Flat silver tinsel in two halves
Hackles: Black cock tied to divide the body and a slightly larger black cock hackle tied in front

The Delphi Silver, an excellent seatrout pattern, is named after the famous Delphi seatrout and salmon fishery, located in the Doo Lough Valley of south-west Mayo. It is at its most effective in clear water. It is essentially a lough fly and fishes equally well by day or by night. Fresh-run seatrout will often be seen to come a long way to intercept it.

Devil

PLATE 3

Hook: Size 8-12 Partridge L2A
Tying silk: Black.

Rib: Fine flat gold tinsel
Body: Black floss silk
Hackle: Black cock
Wing: Grouse tail with a slip of red swan tied over

A traditional lough pattern that will often take a trout when buzzers are hatching by day.

Donegal Blue

PLATE 3

Hook: Size 8-12 Partridge L2A
Tying silk: Black
Rib: Wide flat silver tinsel - two turns.
Body: Dark blue seal's fur
Hackle: Black cock, not too heavy

A Donegal seatrout pattern, very effective in that county for salmon and seatrout, and on loughs further south as well.

Duckfly

PLATE 4

Hook: Size 10-12 Partridge JIA
Tying silk: Black
Rib: Fine silver wire
Body: Black floss silk, tapered
Wing: Two white cock hackle points
Hackle: Black hen tied sparse

When duckfly or black buzzers return to the water to lay their eggs they then drop on to the water and die. This is a good pattern to fish just under the surface in this situation. It will also take trout when duckfly are hatching out.

It is one of the deadliest patterns I know of for daytime river seatrout fishing in Connemara. Fish it dressed on a size 12 hook on a fine leader. It can be fished singly or with one other fly on the leader. Never fish more than two flies in this situation. It should be fished on a dead drift or retrieved

PLATE 5: WET FLIES
Top Row G & H Sedge, Gadget, Ginger Quill
1st Row Goat's Toe, Golden Olive, Goat's Toe (Rush)
2nd Row Grace Kelly, Gold Butcher, Golden Olive Bumble
3rd Row Gosling (Yellow), Gold Ribbed Hare's Ear Nymph, Gosling (Rush)
4th Row Gosling (Grey)
Bottom Row Green Drake, Green Dabbler

with a slow figure-of-eight retrieve in slow pools. A wing consisting of a pinch of white hair from the tip of a grey squirrel tail is preferred for the seatrout pattern and is the one used to such deadly effect by the Galway angler Danny Lydon, at Ballynahinch.

Duckfly Emerger

PLATE 4

Hook: Size: 10-14 Kamasan B160
Tying silk: Black.
Tag: Flat silver tinsel (tied round the bend)
Rib: Silver wire
Body: Black silk
Wings: Two white cock hackle tips
Thorax: Hot orange seal's fur
Hackle: Two turns of black hen

An excellent Cyril Conlon pattern for a duckfly hatch on Lough Corrib and anywhere else where this fly hatches. It is useful in sizes 10, 12 and 14. On occasions, it is dressed without the silver tag, in which case the black silk body should be taken partly round the bend of the hook.

Duckfly Emerger Variant (Cyril Conlon)

PLATE 4

Hook: Size 10-12 Kamasan B160
Tying silk: Black
Rib: Fine silver wire
Body: Black silk taken partly round the bend of the hook
Wings: White cock hackle tips
Thorax: Hot orange seal's fur
Hackle: Brown partridge

Dunkeld

PLATE 4

Hook: Size 8-12 Partridge L2A

Tying silk: Black
Rib: Fine oval gold tinsel.
Tail: Golden pheasant topping
Body: Flat gold tinsel
Hackle: Hot orange cock palmered with a pinch of blue jay tied in at the throat
Wing: Bronze mallard
Eyes: Jungle cock

A good attractor pattern for brown trout when orange buzzers are hatching and in late June when perch fry are about. It is also an excellent pattern for salmon and seatrout in rivers in peat-stained falling water after a spate. When fished for salmon a slip of red swan is set inside the bronze mallard wing.

Dunkeld Nymph

PLATE 4

Hook: Size 10-12 Partridge L2A
Tying silk: Black
Rib: Fine oval gold tinsel
Tail: Golden pheasant topping
Body: Flat gold tinsel
Thorax: Peacock herl
Hackle: Hot orange at throat with blue jay in front
Eyes: Jungle cock

A Dunkeld nymph does not belong in the realm of the insect kingdom but this is a pattern I have found useful when the first shoals of tiny perch fry are seen hovering just beneath the surface in June or early July. It can be cast into the rings of a fry-feeding trout and fished static, but it also takes trout when fished lough-style in any position on the leader.

Dyson

PLATE 4

Hook: Size 8-12 Partridge L2A
Tying silk: Black

Tail: Slip of scarlet quill
Body: Peacock herl
Hackle: Dark red-brown or furnace cock

A North American pattern that was once popular at Burrishoole, fished on the point, for salmon and seatrout.

Extractor

PLATE 4

Hook: Size 8-10 Partridge L2A
Tying silk: Black
Rib: Oval gold tinsel
Tail: A pinch of golden pheasant red breast feathers
Body: Flat gold tinsel
Hackle: Lemon-yellow cock, fairly long and swept back with a good pinch of golden pheasant red breast feather at the throat
Wing: Bronze mallard

A pattern from Rogan of Ballyshannon, this is a good brown trout attractor. It is still much used in the mayfly season and post-mayfly on loughs Sheelin, Erne and Melvin. Usually fished on the point.

Extractor (Cathal Rush)

PLATE 4

Hook: Size 10-12 Partridge G3A
Tying silk: Black
Rib: Gold wire
Tail: Fibres of cock pheasant centre tail
Body: Flat gold tinsel
Hackle: Lemon-yellow cock, under red golden pheasant breast feather, under bronze mallard tied all round.

A consistently good fly, even at mayfly time. It is particularly good for coloured water and works well on Sheelin and Melvin late in the season.

Fanwing Mayfly

PLATE 4

Hook: Size 8-10 Kamasan B830
Tying silk: Brown
Rib: One strand of red floss silk tightly twisted
Tail: About five fibres of cock pheasant centre tail tied slightly longer than the hook shank
Body: Natural raffia, moistened
Wings: Two small mallard drake breast feathers dyed lemon yellow
Hackle: Ginger cock wound behind and in front of the wing

Mayfly patterns are legion. This one is still used very successfully when the duns are hatching on Corrib, Mask, Conn and Carna. It can be fished dry, or on the bob and pulled through the water with a team of wet flies. In the latter case, it is best oiled so that it bobs to the surface and is left sitting there tantalisingly before lift-off.

Fenian

PLATE 4

Hook: Size 8-12, Partridge L2A
Tying silk: Brown
Rib: Oval gold tinsel
Tail: Golden pheasant topping
Body: Rear third, orange floss; front two-thirds emerald green floss
Hackle: Red game, palmered
Wing: Bronze mallard

The Fenian is derived from the old salmon pattern of the same name and was probably first tied as an attractor for trout. Even so, it may still relate to things in nature to some extent, with its two-toned body, and it is an excellent choice on the lough when sedges are hatching on summer evenings. Fish it on the top or middle dropper.

Fiery Brown

PLATE 4

Hook: Size 8-14 Partridge L2A
Tying silk: Brown
Rib: Fine oval gold tinsel
Tail: Golden pheasant tippets
Body: Fiery brown seal's fur
Hackle: Fiery brown cock
Wing: Bronze mallard

If ever there was a fly that proved how versatile and effective traditional wet fly patterns can be, this is it. Fished on the point very early in the season along rocky shores, especially on Lough Conn, it will take trout feeding on freshwater shrimps. Fished on the middle dropper in summer it will be taken for a sedge. In spring it is highly effective fished on the bob during the day, when orange duckfly are hatching.

It is one of the best-known patterns from Rogans of Ballyshannon. Several dressings exist. I find the one given above the simplest and entirely adequate. The secret of obtaining Rogans' shade is lost. I use Veniard's fiery brown dye for the seal's fur and the same dye, with a pinch of Veniard's orange dye added, for the hackle.

Fiery Brown Spider (Owen Warner)

PLATE 4

Hook: Size 10-12 Partridge L2A
Tying silk: Brown
Rib: Fine oval gold and gold wire on size 12
Tail: Golden pheasant tippet
Body: Fiery brown seal's fur
Hackle: A brown partridge hackle, wound full circle

A close relative of the Fiery Brown, this spider pattern is useful as a point fly on loughs in spring time. Owen Warner, of Bantry, recommends it highly, in the smaller size, for fishing the hill loughs of Kerry and west Cork.

Fiery Brown Bumble

PLATE 4

Hook: Size 8-14 Partridge L2A
Tying silk: Brown
Rib: Fine oval gold tinsel
Tail: Indian crow substitute
Body: Fiery brown seal's fur
Hackle: A fiery brown hackle and a blood-red dyed hackle, palmered

Kingsmill Moore recommended this pattern mainly for coloured water. He remarked that he was not quite satisfied with the dressing but was not able to improve on it. That may be so, but it does not prevent it still being a favourite today with those who fish for seatrout in the peat-stained water of western loughs.

Fiery Brown Sedge

PLATE 4

Hook: Size 10 Kamasan 830
Tying silk: Brown
Tag: Yellow floss
Rib: Black tying silk
Body: Fiery brown seal's fur
Wing: A pinch of brown bucktail with two small cree cock hackle points tied one on each side
Hackle: A cree and a red game hackle wound in front of the wing

A pattern for the top dropper when larger sedges such as the cinnamon sedge are about on the lough. It is used on the Midland lakes and I first got the dressing from Liam Gilsenan of Multyfarnham.

PLATE 6: WET FLIES

Top Row Green Hopper (Rush), Grasshopper, Green Olive
1st Row Greenwell's Spider, Green Mayfly, Greenwell's Glory
2nd Row Green & Yellow Nymph (Ivens), Green Peter Pupa
3rd Row Grenadier, Green Peter, Green Nymph (Brown)
4th Row Grouse & Claret, Grey Murrough, Green & Red Buzzer (Brown)
Bottom Row Hackled Golden Olive, Hackled Hare's Ear, Hare's Ear, Hare's Ear & Claret

Fluorescent Green Dabbler (Cathal Rush)

PLATE 4

Hook: Size 8-10 Kamasan B160
Tying silk: Black
Rib: Silver wire
Tail: Tippets dyed hot orange
Body: Globrite green floss (No.9) with pearl tinsel over
Hackle: Black cock, palmered
Wing: Bronze mallard, tied all round

Freshwater Louse (Asellus)

PLATE 4

Hook: Size 10 Kamasan B175
Tying silk: Fine oval gold tinsel
Tail: Fibres of bronze mallard
Shell back: Fibres of hen pheasant centre tail tied in at the tail, taken over the top of the body and tied off at the head
Underbody: A few turns of fine lead wire
Body: Hare's ear with some fawn fur from the mask mixed in
Hackle: Brown partridge, palmered.

The freshwater louse (Asellus) is especially active early in the season (February-March) and it features quite a bit in the lough trout's diet. This is a pattern to be fished on the point, especially in areas where underwater vegetation has died back during the winter. The water louse population can increase greatly if there is much over-winter decay of bottom vegetation due to lack of light caused by eutrophication.

French Partridge Mayfly

PLATE 4

Hook: Size 10 Kamasan B830, or size 8-10 Partridge L2A, or size 8-10 Kamasan B175
Tying silk: Brown
Rib: Fine oval gold
Tail: Four or five fibres of cock pheasant centre tail
Body: Natural raffia, moistened
Body hackle: Short medium-olive cock hackle, palmered
Hackle: Medium-olive cock hackle, rather long in fibre, with a French partridge hackle wound in front

A simple but very effective pattern to be fished on the bob when mayfly are hatching. It is usually fished wet and pulled just under the surface. However, I have seen this pattern oiled up and fished like a dry fly on Lough Corrib.

Freshwater Shrimp (Gammarus)

PLATE 4

Hook: Size 10-12 Partridge JIA
Tying silk: Primrose or golden olive
Rib: Fine gold wire which binds down the PVC strip to give a segmented effect
Tail: Fibres of cree cock hackle.
Shell back: A strip of clear PVC tied in at the tail, stretched over the back and tied down at the head
Body: Golden olive seal's fur, tied round the bend of the hook
Hackle: Cree cock palmered and clipped clean on top of the hook shank
Whisks: A few fibres of cree cock hackle tied in at the head pointing forward

I first tried this pattern in the early eighties for shrimp-feeding trout on Lough Mask. It proved so effective that I never felt any need to alter the dressing except occasionally to add a little fine lead wire to the hook shank for weight. Shrimps are an important food item for both river and lough brown trout. They will take them at any time but I find this pattern works best fished on the point along rocky shores with a good wave on the water, in midsummer. It has taken trout up to 4³/₄lb for me.

Gadget

PLATE 5

Hook: Longshank size 6 heavy wire
Tying silk: Black
Rib: Fine oval silver tinsel
Tail and back: Slips of bronze mallard tied in at the end of the body with the points extending beyond the hook bend and tied over the top of the body
Body: Flat silver tinsel over an underbody of grey floss silk

Usually known as Rogans Gadget, it was first tied for fishing for seatrout on the Erne Estuary at Ballyshannon.

G & H Sedge

PLATE 5

Hook: Size 8-12 Partridge L2A
Tying silk: Olive
Body: Deerhair spun on the silk and tied the length of the hook shank. It is then trimmed to give a sedge silhouette, clipping it very close on the underside
Lower body: Dark green seal's fur spun between a double length of olive tying thread, tied in at the end of the body. This is pulled tight under the body and tied in under the head
Hackle: Red-brown cock hackle trimmed at the top
Antennae (optional): Two stripped hackle stems

A useful pattern for river or lough, devised by John Goddard and Cliff Henry. It has taken several trout late at night on deep pools on the Boyne. Some anglers like to fish it on the point to float a team of buzzer pupae and find that the trout often take the

G & H Sedge out of preference.

Goat's Toe

PLATE 5

Hook: Size 8-12 Partridge L2A
Tying silk: Black
Tail: Red wool
Rib: Red wool twisted tightly
Body: Bronze peacock herl
Hackle: Blue peacock neck feather

A lough pattern for the west of Ireland. It is still popular and more likely to take a salmon than a trout.

Goat's Toe (Cathal Rush)

PLATE 5

Hook: Size 10-12 Kamasan B160
Tying silk: Black
Tag: Flat gold tinsel
Tail and rib: Orange Globrite (No.4) floss
Body: Bronze peacock herl
Hackle: Long black cock under blue peacock neck feather, tied full

This is a dressing for early in the season but it is good for pulling trout up when the fishing is difficult

Gold Butcher

PLATE 5

Hook: Size 8-10 Partridge L2A
Tying silk: Black
Rib: Fine oval gold tinsel
Tail: Red ibis substitute or a slip of red swan
Body: Flat gold tinsel
Hackle: Claret cock
Wing: Slips of blue mallard wing quill.

This is a variation on the standard dressing, which has a black hackle. I prefer the claret hackle and find it an excellent pattern for seatrout in the clear-water western loughs such as Tawnyard and the Delphi loughs. It will take salmon too and I sometimes add two small jungle cock eyes.

Golden Olive

PLATE 5

Hook: Size 8-12 Partridge L2A
Tying silk: Golden olive or brown
Rib: Fine oval gold tinsel
Tail: Golden pheasant topping
Body: Golden olive seal's fur
Hackle: Golden olive or light ginger cock
Wing: Bronze mallard

A traditional pattern, mainly for the lough, which can be called upon at mayfly time, when golden olive buzzers are hatching, and during the autumn hatch of lake olives.

Golden Olive Bumble

PLATE 5

Hook: Size 8-12 Partridge L2A
Tying silk: Brown
Rib: Fine oval gold tinsel
Tail: Golden pheasant crest feather
Body: Golden-olive seal's fur
Hackle: A golden-olive and a medium-red natural cock hackle, palmered
Front hackle: Blue jay

A Kingsmill Moore pattern for the loughs. It really comes into its own at mayfly time. In fact it is almost impossible to visualise a cast of flies at that time of year which would not feature it somewhere - bob, middle or point. This is especially true for the western loughs. Size 10 appears to be the most effective size. A recent variation is to add a small tag of hot orange seal's fur or to incorporate a pinch of hot orange seal's fur at the end of the body. The hackles in the dressing are as given by Kingsmill Moore,

but some prefer a lighter shade of ginger instead of the red game.

Gold-Ribbed Hare's Ear Nymph

PLATE 5

Hook: Size 12-14 Partridge L2A
Rib: Fine flat gold tinsel or fine oval gold tinsel
Tail: A few long fibres of guard hair from a hare's mask
Body: Dark hare's ear fur
Thorax: As body but thicker
Legs: Under part of thorax well teased out with the dubbing brush

Probably the most effective nymph fly an angler could choose to use on a river either early in the season or later on when olives are hatching, especially large dark olives, medium olives, small dark olives, yellow evening duns and caenis. This is one of the few patterns that I can say has caught literally hundreds of trout for me. Yet it looks so inconspicuous in the fly box that you can easily pass over it. Fish it on its own or on the dropper with a team of wet flies. I love the confident way trout take it at the neck of a pool and the sense of surprise caused by a solid take at the end of a glide when you think there are no more trout left in that stretch.

Gosling (Grey)

PLATE 5

Hook: Size 10 Kamasan B830
Tying silk: Brown
Rib: Fine oval gold tinsel
Tail: Fibres of bronze mallard
Body: Golden olive seal's fur
Hackles: Orange cock with dyed yellow mallard flank doubled and wound in front

PLATE 7: WET FLIES

Top Row Hare's Ear & Furnace, Hare's Ear & Woodcock, Heather Moth, Harry Tom
1st Row Invicta, Iron Blue Dun, Hob Nob, Iron Blue Emerger
2nd Row Jacob's Ladder, Jennings Nymph, Jerry-Ma-Diddler
3rd Row Jungle Cock, Johnston, Kate McLaren, Kill Devil Spider
4th Row Kingfisher Butcher, Kingsmill, Lamplighter
Bottom Row Lake Olive Nymphs by Conlon, Kelly, and Harris

Gosling (Yellow)

PLATE 5

Hook: Size 10 Kamasan B830
Tying silk: Brown
Rib: Fine oval gold tinsel
Tail: Four fibres of cock pheasant centre tail
Body: Golden olive seal's fur
Hackles: Hot orange cock with grey mallard flank feather doubled and wound in front

The Gosling appears to have originated in the area of Lough Melvin and Lough Erne. It is especially popular at mayfly time, not only there, but also on the big western brown trout loughs. There are at least a dozen variations but they reduce to two principle dressings: the Yellow Gosling and the Grey Gosling. Goslings can be fished on Lough Melvin all season and will take trout and salmon. They are useful too on loughs Conn and Mask. The grey one is usually fished on the point and the yellow one in any position. The style of dressing can vary depending on whether the fly is tied as a bob fly or further down the leader. The more turns of hackle made in front of the body the more the mallard fibres stand out. Fewer turns, and you get a slimmer, nymph-like fly.

Gosling (Cathal Rush)

PLATE 5

Hook: Size 10-12 Partridge L3A
Tying silk: Golden olive
Rib: Oval gold tinsel
Tail: Cock pheasant centre tail fibres
Body: Golden olive seal's fur
Hackle: Yellow golden pheasant breast feather, under long hot orange cock, under sparse grey mallard flank

This is a dressing that is useful throughout the season and is especially effective for salmon on loughs such as Melvin and Conn.

Grace Kelly

PLATE 5

Hook: Size 8-12 Partridge L2A
Tying silk: Brown
Rib: Fine oval gold tinsel
Tail: A bunch of cock pheasant centre tail fibres
Body: Golden olive seal's fur
Hackle: Ginger cock
Wing: Grey mallard flank dyed lemon yellow

A pattern for Lough Melvin, Lough Conn and the midland lakes at mayfly time.

Grasshopper

PLATE 6

Hook: Size 10 Kamasan B830
Tying silk: Brown
Rib: Fine oval gold tinsel
Tail: A small bunch of bucktail
Body: Insect green seal's fur
Sides: Two cock pheasant church window feathers
Legs: Four pairs of cock pheasant centre tails, each pair knotted together in the middle and tied in on either side, and splayed outwards, to give a kicking action when drawn through the water
Hackle: A green olive and a ginger cock hackle wound together

A pattern to be fished on the bob on the big loughs in a good wave in late July, through August and September.

Green & Red Buzzer (Peter Brown)

PLATE 6

Hook: Size 12-14 Kamasan B175
Tying silk: Red
Rib: Fine flat gold tinsel

Body: Red floss or tying silk
Thorax: Insect green seal's fur
Hackle: Short brown partridge (very sparse)

This pattern was tied to cope with the buzzer hatch that occurs at dusk on Lough Ennell at mayfly time. As buzzers are by no means confined to Ennell, this pattern will surely be useful on other loughs as well.

Green & Yellow Nymph (Tom Ivens)

PLATE 6

Hook: Size 12 Partridge L2A
Tying silk: Brown
Body: Two strands of green swan or goose tail at the rear with two strands of yellow herl wound in front to within an 1/8 of the eye
Head: One or two strands of peacock herl

This pattern has been successful on Lough Sheelin when fished in a light ripple. Trout will take it either for a small sedge pupa or a buzzer pupa. It is not very durable to trouts' teeth, so I usually add a rib of fine clear monofilament for extra strength.

Green Dabbler

PLATE 5

Hook: Size 8-10 Partridge L2A
Tying silk: Black
Rib: Fine oval gold
Tail: Eight fibres of cock pheasant tail tied 1¹/₂ times the length of the body
Body: Pale olive seal's fur
Hackle: Light medium olive cock, palmered
Wing: Bronze mallard tied normal style (as for a wet fly)
Front hackle: Two turns of red-brown cock doubled and tied to lie close to the wing

The Green Dabbler is a variation on the

Dabbler invented by Donald McClarn. It is popular on loughs Corrib and Mask, and in 1993 a Green Dabbler accounted for a 13lb 2oz Corrib trout for Galway City angler Tony Kelly. This is a most useful pattern. It is very effective at mayfly time, on Sheelin and Conn, and continues to take trout right to the end of the season.

Green Drake

PLATE 5

Hook: Size 8-10 Partridge L2A or Size 10 Kamasan B830
Tying silk: Brown
Rib: Oval gold tinsel
Tail: Fibres of cock pheasant centre tail
Body: Natural raffia, moistened
Body hackle : Badger cock palmered with a few turns of medium olive in front
Front hackle: Grey mallard flank dyed green olive

A pattern that can be fished in any position on the leader when mayfly are hatching.

Green Hopper (Cathal Rush)

PLATE 6

Hook: Size 12 Kamasan B160
Tying silk: Olive
Tag: Orange Globrite floss
Rib: Oval gold tinsel
Body: Pale olive seal's fur well picked out
Legs: Cock pheasant centre tail fibres (six pairs) knotted twice near the tips
Hackle: Short ginger cock - dry fly quality

The Green Hopper is always good on the lough from May onwards and it can be fished wet or dry.

Green Mayfly

PLATE 6

Hook: Size 10 Kamasan B830
Tying silk: Brown
Rib: Fine oval gold tinsel
Tail: Four fibres of cock pheasant centre tail
Body: Natural raffia, moistened
Hackle: Medium olive, three turns in front of the body and the remainder palmered
Front hackle: French partridge dyed green olive

An excellent mayfly pattern for the top dropper for Lough Corrib or anywhere when mayflies with a pronounced olive hue are hatching.

Green Nymph (Peter Brown)

PLATE 6

Hook: Size 12-14 Kamasan B175
Tying silk : Green
Body: Green sewing cotton (Gütermann's Shade 616)
Hackle: Black hen or dark partridge

A fly for wherever green buzzers hatch. This one works well on Lough Mask. Fish it on the dropper with another pupa on the point.

Green Olive

PLATE 6

Hook: Size 8-14 Partridge L2A
Tying silk: Brown
Rib: Fine oval gold tinsel
Tail: Golden pheasant tippets
Body: Green olive seal's fur
Hackle: Green olive cock or hen
Wing: Bronze mallard

A traditional pattern that is still useful on acid lakes when olives are hatching. Especially useful for Lough Melvin.

Green Peter

PLATE 6

Hook: Size 8-12 Partridge L2A
Tying silk: Brown or black
Rib: Fine oval gold tinsel
Body: Green olive seal's fur
Hackle: Red game palmered and clipped on the top edge
Wing: Four slips of hen pheasant secondary tied in flat on top of the body so as to partly envelop it - boat-wing style
Head hackle: Red game

If I were asked to nominate the Number 1 lough fly for either brown trout or grilse, it would have to be the Green Peter. It is so effective in deceiving brown trout that it can be fished all season long. It is essentially a sedge pattern which, to the best of my knowledge, originated in the Midlands to represent the big speckled sedges (*Phryganea varia* and *P. obsoleta*). It was originally a dry fly fished at dusk in July/August, but soon its effectiveness as a wet fly was discovered and it is as a wet fly that is now most widely used. It is most often fished on the dropper but is very effective as a point fly at mayfly time, especially on Lough Conn. (A floating dressing is given on p.75)

Its usefulness as a lough salmon fly cannot be over-emphasised especially when the grilse come in. Fish it on the bob. I prefer to dress it for grilse without a body hackle. The Green Peter is an exceptionally effective fly.

Green Peter Pupa

PLATE 6

Hook: Size 8 Partridge GRS6A, or Yorkshire sedge hook
Tying silk: Olive
Rib: Flat silver tinsel

PLATE 8: WET FLIES
Top Row Legs Eleven (Claret), Lansdale Partridge, Legs Eleven (Olive)
1st Row Leonard's Hatching Duckfly, Light Partridge & Yellow,
Lough Arrow Mayfly, Light Olive
2nd Row Mallard & Claret, Lough Erne Gosling, March Brown
3rd Row March Brown Spider, Loch Ordie, Matt Gorman
Bottom Row Mayfly Nymph (Brown) Mayfly Nymph (McTeare)

Back strip: Slip of turkey dyed dark green/olive
Body: Olive green seal's fur tied thick
Wings: Hen pheasant wing tied short along the body
Legs: Fibres of grey and bronze mallard tied underneath and extending beyond the hook bend

Sedge pupae are best tied on sedge hooks with the body starting well around the bend. Green peters hatch in open water at dusk in July-August. The pupae are active for several hours before emerging and trout can be taken in suitable conditions earlier in the evening on an imitation fished on the point.

Greenwell's Glory

PLATE 6

Hook: Size 12-16 Partridge L2A
Rib: Gold wire or fine oval gold tinsel
Tail: Coch-y-bondhu hackle fibres
Body: Yellow tying silk pulled through brown cobbler's wax
Hackle: Greenwell or coch-y-bondhu (sparse)
Wing: Starling

A good top dropper fly for the river especially when large dark olives, medium olives, or small dark olives are hatching. It is a good fly on the lough, too, tied with an olive rayon floss body, when olive buzzers or early-season lake olives are hatching.

Greenwell's Spider

PLATE 6

Hook: Size 14-16 Partridge L2A
Rib: Gold wire or very fine oval tinsel
Body: Yellow tying silk pulled through brown cobbler's wax
Hackle: One and a half or two turns of coch-y-bondhu hen, long in fibre. Some anglers

prefer a woodcock breast hackle tied sparse

The Greenwell's Spider is always a useful pattern for the river fisher who chooses to fish wet when olives are hatching. It will also take trout on the lough during a hatch of lake olives

Grenadier

PLATE 6

Hook: Size 12 Partridge L2A
Tying silk: Orange
Rib: Fine oval gold tinsel
Body: Hot orange seal's fur or floss
Hackle: Two turns of light furnace cock

This English reservoir fly was invented by a Dr Bell for Blagdon Reservoir. I have had requests to tie it for Irish anglers who like to fish it in a hatch of orange buzzers.

Grey Murrough

PLATE 6

Hook: Size 10 Kamasan B830 or Size 8-10 Partridge L2A
Tying silk: Black
Rib: Oval silver tinsel
Body: Grey seal's fur
Wings: Grey speckled hen
Hackle: Red game
Antennae: Two cock pheasant centre tail fibres

A lake pattern for the Midlands usually fished on the dropper in a good wave in August-September.

Grouse & Claret

PLATE 6

Hook: Size 10-12 Partridge L2A
Tying silk: Black
Rib: Fine oval gold tinsel

Tail: Golden pheasant tippet
Body: Claret seal's fur
Hackle: Dark claret cock
Wing: Slips of grouse tail feather

A traditional pattern popular on western and mountain loughs. Useful when dark sedges are about or in a small size during a hatch of claret duns.

Hackled Golden Olive

PLATE 6

Hook: Size 10-12 Partridge L2A
Tying silk: Primrose or golden olive
Rib: Fine oval gold tinsel
Tail: Golden pheasant topping
Body: Spinnaker insect-green dapping floss
Hackle: Golden olive cock, lightly palmered
Wing: Bronze mallard

For those who like to fish traditional-style patterns it is good to have the assurance that a fly works well. This one was tied by James Murphy of Newry to cope with hatches of apple-green midges on Lough Sheelin.

Hackled Hare's Ear

PLATE 6

Hook: Size 10-12 Partridge L2A
Tying silk: Black
Rib: Fine oval gold tinsel
Body: Hare's ear fur
Hackle: Good-quality red game cock, palmered
Wing: Hen pheasant secondary

I never cease to be amazed at the effectiveness of flies dressed with hare's ear in attracting and taking trout. I was first introduced to this fly by Merion Jones of Criccieth, North Wales, who assured me that it was of Irish origin and may well be a Dr Michael Kennedy pattern. It has proved its

worth on both the Midland lakes and Lough Conn from early in the season. It is fished on the top dropper. Trout probably take it for a sedge fluttering on the surface, but it works equally well when lake olives are hatching and will bring up trout even when there are no flies about. Some anglers fish it dry (size 12) in the flat calm and find it extremely effective.

Hare's Ear

PLATE 6

Hook: Size 12-16 Partridge L2A
Tying silk: Brown or olive
Rib: Fine oval or flat gold tinsel
Tail: Guard hairs from a hare's mask or a few fibres of guinea-fowl
Body: Hare's ear fur
Hackle: Body fibres well picked out
Wing: Dark starling

A great fly for river trout especially early in the season when dark olives and medium olives are about. Fish the bigger pattern early and the smaller sizes, 14 or 16, as the season progresses.

Hare's Ear & Claret

PLATE 6

Hook: Size 12-14 Partridge L2A
Tying silk: Black
Rib: Gold wire
Tail: Blue dun hackle fibres
Body: Hare's ear fur
Thorax: Claret seal's fur well picked out
Wing: Starling

This is an old pattern from the upper Erne in Co Cavan. It is a good all-round pattern and is likely to take a trout from streamy water at any time of the season.

Hare's Ear & Furnace

PLATE 7

Hook: Size 12-16 Partridge L2A
Tying silk: Brown
Tag: Flat gold tinsel
Rib: Gold wire or fine flat tinsel
Body: Hare's ear fur
Hackle: One and a half turns of furnace hen hackle

A great little fly for use on the rivers early in the season when olives are likely to be hatching. Fish it on the dropper and work it into the backwaters by the edge, where it can be dibbled at the surface to represent an emerging dun.

Hare's Ear & Woodcock

PLATE 7

Hook: Size 12-16 Partridge L2A
Tying silk: Primrose
Rib: Fine flat gold tinsel
Tail: A few fibres of bronze mallard
Body: Hare's ear fur
Hackle: Body fur well picked out at the thorax
Wing: Slips of woodcock wing quill

This is a variation on the Hare's Ear and is an excellent fly on the loughs in April, May and September when lake olives are hatching.

Harry Tom

PLATE 7

Hook: Size 10-12 Partridge L2A
Tying silk: Brown
Rib: Fine oval silver tinsel
Tail: Honey dun hackle fibres
Body: Rabbit fur and hare's ear mixed
Hackle: Honey dun
Wing: Bronze mallard

An old Welsh pattern, it is still used by brown trout anglers on the limestone loughs during a hatch of lake olives or olive buzzers.

Heather Moth

PLATE 7

Hook: Size 8-12 Partridge L2A
Tying silk: Black
Rib: Fine oval silver tinsel
Tail: Yellow wool
Body: Grey seal's fur
Hackle: Grizzle cock, palmered, with another grizzle hackle wound in front

The Heather Moth is a seatrout fly for the west of Ireland and Connemara fisheries in August and September.

Hob Nob

PLATE 7

Hook: Size 12 Partridge E1A
Tying silk: Black
Rib: Gold wire
Tail: Four fibres of golden pheasant tippet tied long, equal to the length of the hook shank
Body: Bottle-green seal's fur tied slim
Thorax: Mole fur tied small
Hackle: Two turns of short red game

I was first given this pupa pattern at Lough Mask by Jimmy Murphy of Cushlough. He assured me that one of his guests used it there to great effect in May and June when buzzers were hatching. It was usually fished close to the surface in the shelter of an island or on the edge of the ripple.

Subsequent trials proved that to be correct and it was very successful in many of the bays along the east shore of the lough from Cushlough Bay down to Ballinshalla Bay. It can be fished in a buzzer rise during the day but is especially effective at dusk.

Invicta

PLATE 7

Hook: Size 8-12 Partridge L2A
Tying silk : Brown or black
Rib: Fine oval gold tinsel
Tail: Golden pheasant topping
Body: Yellow seal's fur
Hackle: Light red game cock palmered, with a beard hackle of blue jay
Wing: Hen pheasant secondary wing quill slips

This is one of the old reliable patterns for summer and autumn fishing. I have no idea what it represents but trout may well take it for an evening sedge. It is also a useful fly to have at mayfly time, especially on Lough Conn and Lough Melvin. I tend to regard it primarily as a fly for the middle dropper or the point.

Iron Blue Dun

PLATE 7

Hook: Size 14-16 Partridge L2A
Tying silk: Red
Tag: A couple of turns of red tying silk
Tail: Fibres of iron blue cock hackle
Body: Mole's fur or any dark blue-grey poly dubbing
Hackle: Iron blue dun, tied very sparse
Wing: Moorhen or darkest starling

The iron blue dun (*Baetis pumilus*) is of greatest interest to trout in the river in late April, May and June. This is just one of several wet fly imitations. I have also seen this pattern used to take trout on the Midland loughs during an evening hatch of buzzers.

Iron Blue Emerger

PLATE 7

Hook: Size 16, Kamasan B170
Tying silk: Dull purple
Tail: Fibres of iron blue dun hackle
Body: Tying silk varnished or lightly dubbed with mole fur
Hackle: Two turns of hackle from a jackdaws cape

When trout are taking iron blue duns they can sometimes be difficult to take on a high-riding dry pattern.

In this situation, this pattern devised by Dr Michael Kennedy may be just what you require.

Jacob's Ladder

PLATE 7

Hook: Size 8-12 Partridge L2A
Tying silk: Black
Rib: Flat silver tinsel
Tail: Golden pheasant tippets
Body: Magenta seal's fur
Hackle: Black cock
Wing: Bronze mallard

This appears to have been originally a Donegal seatrout pattern, but is now used on the loughs of the west of Ireland. It is particularly favoured pattern by some northern anglers for seatrout at Delphi and I have taken grilse on it on Finlough. It is often fished on the middle dropper.

Jennings Nymph

PLATE 7

Hook: Size 12-14 Partridge JIA
Tying silk: Black
Rib: Fine copper wire
Tail: Fibres of brown partridge hackle
Body: In two halves: rear, light claret seal's

fur; front half, peacock herl
Hackle: Brown partridge

The term 'nymph' is probably a misnomer here as this is really a hackled wet fly. It excels on Lough Corrib as a point fly fished in small sizes early in the season and into the duckfly period.

Jerry-Ma-Diddler

PLATE 7

Hook: Size 8-12 Partridge L2A
Tying silk: Black
Rib: Fine oval gold tinsel
Tail: Slip of scarlet swan or duck quill
Body: Green wool
Hackle: Claret cock
Wing: Brown mottled turkey tail, with a strip of scarlet duck wing quill on either side

Someone commented about this fly that if it does not catch trout it will surely frighten them. It is effective when trout are on perch fry and is highly recommended as a seatrout fly for Lough Currane.

It is usually fished on the point. Originally an American pattern.

Johnston

PLATE 7

Hook: Size 10-14 Kamasan B175
Tying silk: Black
Tag: Orange seal's fur (small)
Rib: Oval gold tinsel
Tail: Golden pheasant topping
Body: Dark olive and brown olive seal's fur mixed in equal parts
Hackle: Natural black hen - two turns
Wing: Bronze mallard

The Johnston is a fly to rival even the Sooty Olive, especially at duckfly time or when olive buzzers are hatching. It is most

effective tied on a size 12 hook and has got great results on Sheelin, Ennell and Corrib. It was originally tied by the Revd Derek Johnston of Belturbet for the duckfly hatch on Sheelin.

Jungle Cock

PLATE 7

Hook: Size 10-12 Partridge L2A
Tying silk: Black
Rib: Gold wire
Body: Black floss silk
Hackle: Black cock
Wing: Two jungle cock eyes tied back to back

This is a traditional lough fly. A better known (but in my view inferior) pattern is probably the Jungle Cock & Silver, which is as above but with a silver wire rib and flat silver body.

Kate McLaren

PLATE 7

Hook: Size 10-14 Partridge L2A
Tying silk: Black
Rib: Fine flat silver tinsel
Tail: Golden pheasant topping
Body: Black seal's fur
Hackle: Black cock palmered over the seal's fur and a natural red hen hackle wound in front

This Scottish loch fly from Loch Hope has been found to be equally at home on an Irish Midland limestone lough or on a west of Ireland salmon and seatrout lough. It is a popular choice for brown trout when sedges are about and it is also used for grilse at Burrishoole. Fish it on the top dropper.

PLATE 9: WET FLIES
Top Row Medium Olive Nymph, Mayfly (Rush), Mickey Finn
1st Row Mill's Special, Millerman
2nd Row Murray's Duckfly Emerger, Millar's Sedge (Rush), Mini Bumble
3rd Row Murrough (Claret), Olive Buzzer Pupa, Olive Nymph (Brown), Murrough (Pupa)
4th Row Olive Quill, Orange Grouse, Orange Pupa (Harris), Orange Rail
Bottom Row Paisley, Paisley Pupa, Pearly Black Nymph (Conlon), Perch Fry

Kill Devil Spider

PLATE 7

Hook: Size 10-14 Partridge L2A
Tying silk: Black
Rib: Fine oval silver tinsel
Tail: Dark furnace cock
Body: Rear third flat silver tinsel; front two-thirds, bronze peacock herl
Hackle: Dark Furnace cock

A very popular seatrout fly for the Wicklow and Wexford rivers. Fish it on the point. The smaller sizes are sometimes tied with oval silver for the rear half of the body and in Wexford a blue hackle is occasionally used and makes an attractive and effective fly.

Kingfisher Butcher

PLATE 7

Hook: Size 10-12 Partridge L2A
Tying silk: Black
Rib: Oval gold tinsel
Tail: A slip of kingfisher blue feather
Body: Flat gold tinsel
Hackle: Orange cock
Wing: Slips of slate-coloured mallard primary wing feather

A Scottish fly that is sometimes used as an attractor fly on the loughs.

Kingsmill

PLATE 7

Hook: Size 8-12 Partridge L2A
Tying silk: Black
Tag (for seatrout): Gentian blue floss
Rib: Fine oval silver
Tail: Golden pheasant topping
Body: Black ostrich herl
Hackle: Good-quality black cock
Wing: Crow secondary, rolled tight and tied low over body, with a golden pheasant topping tied in over the top
Eye: Jungle cock (small and not too white)

The Kingsmill, as the name suggests, was first tied by the late T.C. Kingsmill Moore. He describes it as a remarkably good fly for brown trout, seatrout and low-water fishing for salmon. I wholeheartedly concur. It is interesting to note that it was this fly that started me off fly tying. I was given a pattern by Maureen Lyons at Lough Sheelin in the early 1970s. She and her late husband Ally Lyons used it to great effect to take trout feeding on big black buzzers at dusk and dawn in the summer months. It has never been out of my box since and is still in great demand. As the inventor suggests, it can be fished with confidence for trout and salmon. A really good fly.

Lake Olive Nymph (Cyril Conlon)

PLATE 7

Hook: Size 12 Kamasan B160
Tying silk: Brown
Rib: Fine oval gold tinsel
Tail: A small Greenwell hen hackle tip equal to length of hook shank
Body: Pimrose or pale golden olive floss
Hackle: Short badger cock tied sparse

Trout feeding on emerging lake olives can be notoriously difficult. Here, at least, is one pattern that you can try with confidence when faced with this situation. Well proven in the field on Lough Corrib.

Lake Olive Nymph (J.R.Harris)

PLATE 7

Hook: Size 14 Partridge L2A
Tying silk: Golden olive or primrose

Rib: Fine oval gold tinsel or gold wire
Tail: Fibres of grey mallard flank dyed picric or lemon yellow
Body: Pale golden olive seal's fur or hare's ear and yellow seal's fur mixed in equal parts
Wing cases: A slip of any dark brown feather
Thorax: Pale golden olive seal's fur
Hackle: The seal's fur thorax picked out or a few fibres as for the tail

This is a dressing given to me by the late J. R. Harris. He claimed it worked well for him and that it took trout to 5lb on Lough Sheelin. It is cast in the path of a feeding trout and not moved.

Lake Olive Nymph (Michael Kelly)

PLATE 7

Hook: Size 10-12 Kamasan B175
Tying silk: Brown
Rib: Fine copper wire
Tail: Fibres of medium olive dyed hackle
Body: Rear half, medium olive seal fur substitute; front half, hare's ear
Hackle: Medium olive cock tied short

A pattern tied by Michael Kelly of Balbriggan for trout taking lake olives on Lough Ennell. It is usually fished on the point.

Lamplighter

PLATE 7

Hook: Size 8-12 Kamasan B175, B830, or Partridge N1A
Tying silk: Black
Tag: Red and green Glo-Brite floss
Rib: Copper wire and pearl Mylar
Body: Three strands of dyed magenta peacock herl
Hackle: Dark red-brown or dark coch-y-bondhu cock

A dressing by John Horsfall of Bristol for coloured water or loughs with an algal bloom. It is fished on the point and has got some good results for anglers on Lough Conn when other flies were not moving anything. Other suggested Glo-Brite combinations for the tag are shade numbers 1/7, 5/12, 14/15 and 11/13.

Lansdale Partridge

PLATE 8

Hook: Size 10 Kamasan B830
Tail: Fibres of cock pheasant tail
Body: Brown wool
Hackles: Ginger cock with a natural French partridge wound in front

This is a Mayfly pattern for the lakes, especially Melvin and Arrow. Usually fished on the point, where it is likely to take a salmon. It was a particular favourite of the late Canon Patrick Gargan from Cavan for salmon on Lough Melvin, Lough Furnace and Lough Feeagh.

Large Dark Olive Nymph

see Gold-Ribbed Hare's Ear Nymph

Legs Eleven (Claret)

PLATE 8

Hook: Size 10 Partridge L2A
Tying silk: Black
Rib: Fine oval gold tinsel
Tail: Golden pheasant crest feather
Body: Claret seal's fur
Hackle: Claret cock palmered, with two turns of magenta cock in front
Legs: Two lots of five fibres of cock pheasant centre tail knotted as one and tied in on either side
Head hackle: Three turns of blue jay

This is a good all-year-round pattern for

brown trout and it will take grilse too. Fish it on the bob and pull the legs along the surface before lift-off. It was given to me by Michael Kelly of Balbriggan.

Legs Eleven (Olive)

PLATE 8

Hook: Size 10 Partridge L2A
Tying silk: Golden olive
Rib: Fine oval gold tinsel
Body: Pale olive seal's fur
Legs: Three fibres of cock pheasant centre tail knotted as one and tied in either side of the body
Hackle: Grey or brown partridge

A variant of the Claret Legs Eleven. It is a useful fly when trout are taking freshwater shrimps, especially in the early season. It works particularly well in oily water. The knot on the legs should be positioned opposite the bend of the hook.

Leonard's Hatching Duckfly

PLATE 8

Hook: Size 12 Tiemco 2457
Tying silk: Brown
Body: Flat silver tinsel overlaid with clear PVC
Wing: White-tipped grey squirrel tail
Thorax: Three turns of short black ostrich herl with three turns of red ostrich herl wound in front
Head: Red varnish

A pattern of the late Joe Leonard of Cong for Lough Corrib. This dressing was considered revolutionary for its time and proved a great taker of trout both on the Corrib and Midland lakes where duckfly were emerging during the day.

Light Olive

PLATE 8

Hook: Size 12-16 Partridge L2A
Tying silk: Olive
Tail: Pale olive cock hackle fibres
Body: Peacock quill dyed olive
Hackle: Pale olive cock
Wing: Starling

A good early-season pattern for the river and equally good on the loughs in a hatch of olive buzzers.

Light Partridge & Yellow (Peter Brown)

PLATE 8

Hook: Size 14-16 Kamasan B170 or B175
Tying silk: Yellow
Body: Yellow tying silk
Hackle: Grey partridge

A pattern for the summer months when pale olives are hatching on the river. Try fishing it on the point.

Loch Ordie

PLATE 8

Hook: Size 6-14 longshank
Tying silk: Black
Hackles: As many red-brown cock hackles as the hook shank will hold, leaving enough space at the head for two white hackles. It is sometimes tied with a range of different shades of hackle from black at the back, through red brown, red game, ginger, cree, honey and white in front.

The Loch Ordie is a fly for the summer and autumn. It is primarily thought of as being tied in the larger sizes for dapping. It is certainly very useful in this role, especially for seatrout in August and September. The seatrout, especially in the clearer loughs, love the really big flies, well oiled and danced across the wave. In smaller sizes it is useful as a top dropper pattern for both brown trout and seatrout.

Lough Erne Gosling

PLATE 8

Hook: Size 8-10 Kamasan B830
Tying silk: Brown
Rib: Fine oval gold tinsel
Tail: Fibres of bronze mallard
Body: Golden olive seal's fur
Hackle: Scarlet or bright claret cock with a long-fibred grey mallard flank feather dyed golden olive and wound in front

A dressing given by E.J. Malone in his book *Irish Trout and Salmon Flies* and attributed to Sam Anderson.

Lough Arrow Mayfly

PLATE 8

Hook: Size 8 Kamasan B175
Tying silk: Brown
Rib: Fine oval gold tinsel
Tail: Three fibres of cock pheasant centre tail
Body: Natural raffia
Hackle: Good-quality short badger cock, palmered closely, with French partridge dyed green-drake in front, and grey partridge dyed lemon-yellow in front of the French partridge

Frankie McPhillps, the Fermanagh flytyer, regards this as a very good general pattern for Lough Arrow and Lough Erne. It originated in Boyle, Co. Roscommon. Mainly fished on the top dropper.

Mallard & Claret

PLATE 8

Hook: Size 8-14 Partridge L2A
Tying silk: Black
Rib: Fine oval gold tinsel
Tail: Golden pheasant tippets
Body: Claret seal's fur
Hackle: Claret, black, red-brown or ginger cock, according to preference
Wing: Bronze mallard

This is a fly you will find in most lough fishers' fly boxes. It is a very old traditional pattern that represents nothing in particular and yet will take trout right through the season. It is especially useful for early season duckfly hatches and later when sedges are about. Also useful when claret duns are hatching in the bog bays of limestone lakes. Finally, try it late in the season on swollen spate rivers. When tying this pattern, make sure that the wing lies as close as possible on top of the body.

March Brown

PLATE 8

Hook: Size 10-12 Partridge L2A
Tying silk: Golden olive
Rib: Fine oval gold tinsel
Tail: Three fibres of bronze mallard
Body: Hare's ear well picked out
Hackle: Brown partridge
Wing: Partridge tail or hen pheasant secondary

The March Brown is a good early-season lough pattern and is probably taken for a water louse (*Asellus*) by the trout. It can be fished in any position on the leader. It is also a very useful pattern on the river in the smaller sizes, when no flies are hatching. A rib is not necessary in the smaller sizes. However, if the river is coloured after rain, a fine fluorescent green floss rib appears to add to the effectiveness of this fly.

Matt Gorman

PLATE 8

Hook: Size 10-12 Kamasan B175
Tying silk: Brown
Tag: Pale blue floss silk
Rib: Fine oval silver
Body: Bronze peacock herl
Hackle: Red game, palmered
Wing: Hen pheasant secondary
Horns: Fibres of hen pheasant centre tail, two married either side

A fly for the lakes of Killarney. It has a good reputation as a general pattern and is said to take trout when sedges, olives or beetles are about.

Mayfly (Cathal Rush)

PLATE 9

Hook: Size 8 Kamasan B175
Tying silk: Brown
Rib: Bright red thread
Tail: Three fibres of cock pheasant centre tail
Body: Natural seal's fur
Hackle: White cock palmered with a lemon-yellow dyed cock hackle in front and a French partridge hackle dyed golden olive at the head

This is a dressing by Cathal Rush of Armagh. It has proved to be a great taker of trout on loughs Corrib, Mask, Carra and Erne.

Mickey Finn

PLATE 9

Hook: Size 8-10 Partridge L2A
Tying silk: Black
Rib: Fine oval silver tinsel

Body: Flat silver tinsel
Wing: Yellow, scarlet, and yellow bucktail
Eyes: Jungle cock.

A 'last hope' attractor pattern for the lough. Sometimes used for fry-feeding trout. It is also effective on hill loughs.

Mayfly Nymph (Stuart McTeare)

PLATE 8

Hook: Size 8 Longshank Partridge SH3 or Kamasan B830
Tying silk: Brown
Rib: Fine flat gold tinsel
Tail: Cock pheasant tail tips tied short
Body: Hare's body fur well mixed
Wing case: Cock pheasant tail fibres
Thorax: As body
Legs: Thorax and body well picked out

This is a mayfly nymph tied by Stuart McTeare of Finea for Lough Sheelin. He fishes it on the point of a three-fly cast and it has taken trout up to 7lb 13oz for him.

Mayfly Nymph (Peter Brown)

PLATE 8

Hook: Size 8 longshank, Kamasan B830
Tying silk: Brown-olive
Rib: Fine oval gold tinsel (or fine flat gold)
Underbody: 5-amp fuse wire built up to a nymph shape
Tail: Fibres of grey-brown mallard
Body: Hare's ear
Wing case: Dark brown turkey
Hackle: Brown partridge

A mayfly nymph pattern that has been well proved on both river and lake. It can be fished on its own or on the point of a three-fly cast.

Millerman

PLATE 9

Hook: Size 12-14 Kamasan B170
Tying silk: Black
Rib: Fine silver wire
Body: Black floss (marabou)
Hackle: Two turns of badger hen

An excellent pattern when the duckfly females go back on the water to oviposit. They then die and fall on the water and some get trapped in the surface film and sink slowly. Fish this on a fine leader, close to the surface, or cast it in front of feeding trout in sheltered bays, calm patches or on the edge of a ripple.

Millar's Sedge (Cathal Rush)

PLATE 9

Hook: Size 12 Kamasan B170
Tying silk: Brown
Rib: Gold wire wound closely
Tail: Fibres of red-brown cock hackle
Body: None
Hackle: A medium olive cock hackle palmered at the rear of the hook and a red-brown cock hackle palmered in front of it
Wing: Hen pheasant centre tail tied long

This pattern is tied only in small sizes. It can be fished wet or dry and is especially good on bright days. It can be fished on the dropper at mayfly time.

Medium Olive Nymph

PLATE 9

Hook: Size 14 Kamasan B175
Tying silk: Olive
Rib: Gold wire
Tail: Fibres of grey partridge dyed lemon yellow
Body: Hare's ear and yellow seal's fur mixed in equal parts
Wing cases: Any brown feather
Thorax: As body
Hackle: Fibres of grey partridge dyed lemon yellow and tied in at the throat

A nymph for the river early in the season when medium olives (*Baetis tenax*) and small dark olives (*Baetis scambus*) are about. The nymphs of the medium olive and small dark olive can be particularly prevalent in limestone rivers in April and May. At such times try the above. A small Gold-ribbed Hare's Ear Nymph can be used also, fished upstream.

Mini Bumble

PLATE 9

Hook: Size 14 Kamasan B160
Tying silk: Black
Rib: Gold wire
Tail: Golden pheasant topping tied short
Body: Claret seal's fur
Hackle: Short claret cock, palmered.

A fly for the lough in summer or autumn in a small ripple or calm conditions. Fish it on a fine leader and allow it to sink, twitching it occasionally. Trout will take it on the drop. Works best in clear water.

Murrough (Claret)

PLATE 9

Hook: Size 8-10 Partridge L2A
Tying silk: Black
Rib: Fine oval gold tinsel
Body: Claret seal's fur
Hackle: Red-brown cock, palmered
Wing: Dark brown speckled hen or brown turkey
Front hackle: Red-brown cock

The Claret Murrough is a favourite top-dropper fly (and sometimes fished on the point too) for anglers who like to fish traditional lough style in a wave when sedges are about. It can be fished either small or big, depending on the fishing conditions. Anglers have preferences for different shades but they are basically all just shades of claret seal's fur, from medium to dark claret, with a natural red game, red-brown or furnace cock hackle. It is a special favourite on Lough Mask.

Murrough Pupa

PLATE 9

Hook: Size 6-8 Partridge 6 RS 6A
Tying silk: Orange
Rib: Flat gold tinsel
Back: 1/4-inch-wide slip of brown turkey
Body: Fiery brown, orange, medium olive and hare's ear mixed in equal parts and tied thick
Wings: Slips of woodcock tied short
Legs: Long fibres of dark Greenwell hen hackle

Trout sometimes take as many sedge pupae as they do adults. This is a pattern for the murrough hatch, which can occur on loughs any time between late May and August.

Murray's Duckfly Emerger

PLATE 9

Hook: Size 12-14 Kamasan B160
Tying silk: Black
Rib: Fine oval silver tinsel
Body: Flat silver tinsel
Thorax: Orange seal's fur
Hackle: Brown partridge

This is a Cyril Murray pattern for Lough Corrib. It is usually fished on the middle dropper and is especially useful in bright sunny conditions when trout are taking emerging duckfly.

March Brown Spider

PLATE 8

Hook: Size 12-14 Kamasan B170
Tying silk: Brown
Rib: Gold wire
Tail: Fibres of speckled brown partridge
Body: Dark hare's ear fur mixed (4:1) with a pinch of claret seal's fur
Hackle: Brown speckled partridge tied sparse

The natural March Brown hatches in April and May. Trout appear to prefer the nymph to the dun. Fish this pattern either upstream, or down and across, when the naturals are on the water. I have seen good hatches on the Slaney and J.R. Harris says that they also occur on the Liffey, Dodder and Nore.

Mills Special

PLATE 9

Hook: Size 12 Partridge L2A
Tying silk: Black
Rib: Fine flat silver tinsel
Tail: Golden pheasant topping
Body: Red floss
Hackle: Black cock
Eyes: Jungle cock

This pattern is tied by Frankie McPhillips, the noted Fermanagh flytyer. It is chiefly a seatrout pattern and it gained its reputation for the fine bags of seatrout it took at the Erriff and Delphi fisheries, especially on the pools of the Bundorragha River, for the Mills family from Benburn, Co. Tyrone.

Olive Quill

PLATE 9

Hook: Size 12-16 Kamasan B175
Tying silk: Olive

PLATE 10: WET FLIES
Top Row Peter Ross, Petrol Blue, Pheasant Tail Nymph, Priest
1st Row Purcell's Peter, Quail's Fancy, Raymond
2nd Row Raymond Variant, Rayon Floss Shrimp, Red Arrow, Red Sooty Olive
3rd Row Red Spinner, Red Daddy, Red Tag
Bottom Row Red Wickham, Ringrose Pupa, Rough Olive, River Olive

Tail: Fibres of medium olive cock
Body: Peacock eye quill dyed olive
Hackle: Medium olive cock
Wing: Starling

An old favourite, usually associated with the rivers but also an excellent pattern to try on the lough when buzzers are hatching.

Orange Pupa (J.R.Harris)

PLATE 9

Hook: Size 10-12 Kamasan B170
Tying silk: Orange
Tag: Flat silver tinsel
Rib: Brown tying silk (or fine oval silver)
Body: Orange floss silk (Pearsall's marabou)
Thorax: Peacock herl
Wing case: Small jungle cock tied under the thorax.
Hackle: Badger cock tied sparse

This is one of the really great chironomid pupa patterns and is especially effective when the duckfly or orange buzzers are hatching. It is a variant of a pattern devised by J.R. Harris. The shade and brand of floss silk for the body is important as it must turn a deep orange colour when wet. Usually fished on the point and a great favourite on both Lough Corrib and Lough Sheelin.

Olive Nymph (Peter Brown)

PLATE 9

Hook: Size 14-16 Kamasan B170
Tying silk: Yellow
Tail: Fibres of brown partridge tied short
Underbody: 5-amp fuse wire built up to a nymph shape at the thorax
Body: Yellow tying silk
Thorax: Hare's ear
Hackle (optional): Fibres of brown partridge

It is important that a nymph should sink quickly, especially in the river, and this pattern is designed to do just that. Most nymphs are pretty drab in colour and this one fits the bill nicely. It is a good general pattern for either river or lake.

Olive Buzzer Pupa

PLATE 9

Hook: Size 12 Kamasan B170
Tying silk: Olive
Rib: Silver wire
Tail: White cock hackle fibres, tied short
Body: Veniard's olive rayon floss
Wing Case: Cock pheasant centre tail fibres
Thorax: Hare's ear, tied small
Hackle: Badger hen, tied sparse

I first tied this pattern for the May-June hatches of buzzers on Lough Sheelin in the early seventies. It proved very effective and took a lot of trout, especially when fished on a fine leader.

Orange Grouse

PLATE 9

Hook: Size 10-14 Partridge L2A
Tying silk: Orange
Rib: Fine flat or oval gold tinsel
Tail: Fibres of grouse hackle
Body: Orange floss silk
Hackle: Grouse
Wing: Slips of grouse primary

The Orange Grouse I have found to be most effective if stoneflies are observed on the lough. Fish it on the top or middle dropper. Otherwise it is a well-tried traditional pattern and is especially useful on loughs in the south-west. On the river, it is a useful fly when fished in small sizes on the middle dropper when the water is beginning to clear after a flood.

Orange Rail

PLATE 9

Hook: Size 10-14 Kamasan B170
Tying silk: Orange
Body: Orange floss or tying silk, built up
Hackle: Red game
Wing: Cinnamon hen wing quill slips

A pattern for the river to be fished in the runs when sedges are about on summer evenings. There are a whole series of rail flies, so called because many of them used slips of cinnamon landrail (corncrake) wing quill in the wing. E. J. Malone lists eleven Rail dressings in his work *Irish Trout and Salmon Flies*.

Paisley

PLATE 9

Hook: Size 10-12 Partridge L2A
Tying silk: Black
Rib: Fine oval gold tinsel
Body: Light olive seal's fur sparsely dubbed
Hackle: Three badger cock hackles: one white-tipped; one cream-tipped; and one biscuit-yellow. A short blood-red (dyed) cock hackle is wound in front

This is an excellent top-dropper fly when buzzers are hatching. It has a wonderful propensity to pull up a trout when everything else has failed. It is successful even when only a few buzzers are seen on the water and has worked well on loughs Sheelin, Owell, Ennell and Conn. When tying, it is important to sweep the body hackle well back by pressing between thumb and index finger. This was a fly without a name till it was given one by the Preston brothers from Northern Ireland on Lough Sheelin in light hearted banter replying to Southerners who were lauding the effectiveness of the Fenian.

Paisley Pupa

PLATE 9

Hook: Size 12 Kamasan B170
Tying silk: Black
Rib: Gold wire
Body: Dark olive seal's fur tied around the bend of the hook
Hackle: Two turns of badger hen with cream tips
Head: Red seal's fur

A pattern that is obviously related to the wet fly of the same name. It is a good pupa imitation for taking wild trout in late spring and early summer when olive buzzers are hatching.

Pearly Black Nymph (Cyril Conlon)

PLATE 9

Hook: Size 12 Kamasan B160
Tying silk: Black
Rib: Strand of pearl Lureflash
Body: Black seal's fur
Eyes: Small jungle cock by the side of the body
Hackle: Natural black hen tied in front, sparse and swept underneath the body

A really good fly, fished on the point, when buzzers or duckfly are hatching.

Perch Fry

PLATE 9

Hook: Size 8-10 according to size of fry
Tying silk: Pale olive
Rib: Fine oval silver
Tail: Golden pheasant crest
Body: White ribbon material or white silk
Hackle: A pinch of red hackle at the throat
Wing: Two grizzle hackles over two medium

olive hackles tied to lie close along the body

This is a good fish-fry imitation which is best fished, in the area where trout are taking perch fry, in short fast darts. It is just one of a number of flies that work in this situation and the Claret Dabbler, Silver Dabbler and Baby Doll are all excellent flies for taking fry-feeding trout.

Peter Ross

PLATE 10

Hook: Size 8-14 Partridge L2A
Tying silk: Black
Rib: Fine oval silver tinsel or silver wire on small patterns
Tail: Golden pheasant tippets
Body: In two halves: flat silver tinsel, at the rear and red seal's fur in front
Hackle: Black cock
Wing: Teal flank

The Peter Ross has stood the test of time, well-loved by some anglers and loathed by others. It certainly has its good points. In small sizes, especially size 14, it has few equals fished on the dropper at dusk when duckfly are hatching. It often amazes me how they can see it and pick it out. It is useful at perch fry time and is a good fly when seatrout first come into the river or lough.

Petrol Blue (Cyril Conlon)

PLATE 10

Hook: Size 12 Kamasan B160
Tying silk: Brown
Rib: Fine oval gold tinsel
Body: Claret seal's fur tied partly round the bend of the hook
Hackle: Blue jay tied sparse at the throat only
Wing: Bronze mallard tied sparse

An early-season pattern which is best fished on the point in areas where duckfly and other chironomids are hatching.

Pheasant Tail Nymph (Frank Sawyer)

PLATE 10

Hook: Size 12-16 Kamasan B175

Only two materials are required to tie this nymph - four fibres of deep red cock pheasant tail fibres from a mature bird and fine copper wire. The copper wire is first wound on the hook to give a nymph shape. Then tie in the cock pheasant fibres with the wire using the tips for the tail. Wind both fibres and wire to the eye of the hook, secure the fibres with the wire and then form a thorax with the remainder of the fibres and tie off with two half-hitches of the wire.

A popular pattern on the English chalk streams It will take trout here too, especially in small sizes at blue-winged olive time.

Priest

PLATE 10

Hook: Size 10-14, Partridge L2A
Tying silk: Black
Rib: Silver wire
Tail: Red ibis substitute
Body: Flat silver tinsel
Hackle: Badger hen

A pattern for small loughs and even the river when trout are feeding on fish fry.

Purcell's Peter

PLATE 10

Hook: Size 8-12 Kamasan B 170

Tying silk: Black
Rib: Fine oval gold tinsel
Body: Green olive and golden olive seal's fur mixed in equal parts with a pinch of yellow seal's fur added. Pick out with Velcro brush or a dubbing needle
Hackle: Ginger cock, long in fibre
Wing: Hen pheasant secondary

This fly is the creation of Eddie Purcell of Mullingar and is regarded as a marvellously effective pattern by all who fish it.

It is usually fished on the top dropper and some anglers fish a small one on the point. It will take trout right through the season and is especially effective on loughs Ennell and Conn at mayfly time. Eddie thinks that a small thorax of claret seal's fur improves its effectiveness at duckfly time. It will also take salmon and once accounted for seven spring salmon in a day on Carrowmore Lake in Mayo. A feature of this fly is that the hackle is doubled and tied in before the wing, unlike most sedge patterns.

Quail's Fancy

PLATE 10

Hook: Size 10 Kamasan B160
Tying silk: Black
Rib: Fine oval gold tinsel
Tail: Fibres of golden pheasant red spear feather
Body: Dark bottle-green seal's fur
Hackle: Natural black cock palmered with a second hackle tied in front

This is a dressing by Billy Quail. He describes it as an exceptionally good fly for the top dropper on dull days early in the season. He fishes it in preference to a Bibio at such times.

Raymond

PLATE 10

Hook: Size 8-12 Partridge L2A
Tying silk: Brown
Rib: Fine oval gold tinsel
Tail: Golden pheasant tippets
Body: Pale golden olive seal's fur
Hackle: Scarlet cock palmered, with blue jay at the throat
Wing: Hen pheasant secondary, with slips of red and yellow swan between them

A traditional lough fly, the Raymond can be used from mid-season onwards. It is a useful 'last hope' at mayfly time, fished in the middle. Later in the season it is probably taken for an emerging sedge and is certainly very useful for both brown and seatrout.

Raymond Variant

PLATE 10

Hook: Size 8-12 Partridge L2A
Tying silk: Olive
Rib: Fine oval gold tinsel
Tail: Golden pheasant crest
Body: Yellow seal's fur
Hackle: Crimson cock palmered, with one turn of short French partridge dyed green-olive followed by a turn of grey mallard in front, and blue jay at the throat
Wing: Hen pheasant secondary
Front hackle: One and a half turns of grey partridge dyed lemon yellow

Ask an angler what fly he or she used to take a good catch of trout on a lough and you may well be told that it was the Raymond. However, if you get a glimpse of the fly, it is plain to see that it is no ordinary Raymond. This very effective variant, attributed to Murt Folan of Galway, is used on both the western and Midland loughs to great effect. It can be fished from mayfly time right to the end of the season for both brown trout and seatrout.

Red Tag

PLATE 10

Hook: Size 12-14 Kamasan B175
Tying silk: Brown
Tail: Red wool
Body: Peacock herl
Hackle: Red game cock or hen

A wet fly for the river. It is most effective fished on the point when the water is fining down after a flood.

Rayon Floss Shrimp (Cyril Conlon)

PLATE 10

Hook: Size 10-12 Kamasan B160
Tying silk: Black
Rib: Fine oval gold tinsel
Tail: Orange rayon floss, teased out
Body: Orange rayon floss tied chunky
Hackle: Pale ginger or cree cock, palmered
Head: Black

A useful early-season pattern fished on the point in shallow water.

Red Spinner

PLATE 10

Hook: Size 12-16 Kamasan B170
Tying silk: Crimson
Rib: Fine gold wire
Tail: Fibres of blue dun cock
Body: Crimson tying silk
Wings: Two blue dun cock hackle tips tied in a V shape
Hackle: Dull blue dun cock or hen tied sparse

An early-season pattern when large dark

olive spinners are returning to the water. The dead flies are carried downstream under the water surface. Fish it on the top dropper in the early afternoon.

Red Arrow (Syl Higgins)

PLATE 10

Hook: Size 12-16 Partridge L2A
Tying silk: Black
Rib: Fine oval silver tinsel
Tail: Golden pheasant tippets
Body: In two halves, red seal's fur at the the rear and black seal's fur in front
Hackle: Short natural black hen tied sparse
Eyes (optional): Small jungle cock

The Red Arrow is the invention of Syl Higgins, a Longford dentist. It is deadly for lough trout when fished on the point on a floating or slow-sinking line early in the season, just before the duckfly hatch peaks. Syl uses a variation of the Red Arrow for seatrout which has hot orange seal's fur instead of the red. He once took 39 seatrout and 2 salmon on it on the Oweniny River in Mayo and it has taken over 20 seatrout for him on several occasions. The jungle cock eyes were added by me and I think they enhance the original for early-season brown trout.

Red Sooty Olive

PLATE 10

Hook: Size 10-12 Kamasan B175
Tying silk: Black
Rib: Gold wire
Tail: Golden pheasant tippets
Body: Rear two-thirds, sooty olive seal's fur (brown-olive and dark-olive in equal parts); front third, red seal's fur
Hackle: Sooty olive cock
Wing: Bronze mallard

A pattern that was given to me by my colleague, Dr. Paddy Gargan. Very useful when buzzers are hatching on the lough, it works extremely well on Sheelin.

Red Wickham

PLATE 10

Hook: Size 12 Kamasan B175
Tying silk: Black
Rib: Gold wire
Tail: Fibres of red game cock
Body: Flat gold tinsel
Hackle: Red game tied sparse
Wing: Starling
Head: Red varnish

This is a pattern of Seamus Dowds of Kells, Co. Meath, and he frequently ties it on a wee double, size 12. It is a great evening fly for river trout in July and August when fished in the runs and has proved quite effective for seatrout in Donegal.

Red Daddy

PLATE 10

Hook: Size 8-10 Partridge L2A
Tying silk: Black
Rib: Fine oval silver tinsel
Body: Red Lurex
Legs: Six fibres of cock pheasant centre tail, knotted in the middle
Hackle: Claret cock, long in fibre

This is a pattern for seatrout and salmon on the loughs and is attributed to Vincent O'Reilly of Headford. It can be fished on either the dropper or the point and is popular at Lough Inagh, Delphi and the Burrishoole Fishery.

River Olive

PLATE 10

Hook: Size 12-14 Kamasan B175
Tying silk: Yellow
Rib: Gold wire
Tail: Fibres of dark olive cock hackle
Body: Hare's ear fur
Hackle: Cock hackle dyed olive
Wing: Starling primary

A well-proven river pattern from Dr Michael Kennedy. It can be fished either in the streamy water or on the rippled pools. An alternative dressing for the body is to omit the rib and hare's ear fur and use stripped peacock eye quill, but I prefer the original dressing. A fly for the top dropper.

Ringrose Pupa

PLATE 10

Hook: Size 12 Partridge E1A
Tying silk: Black
Rib: 4 lb dark Maxima monofilament
Body: Four heron wing fibres dyed olive (in picric acid)
Thorax: Black floss (tied small)
Hackle: Two turns of short badger hen

Any examination of the stomach contents of lough trout feeding on duckfly pupae will reveal that a large percentage of them are olive in colour. This is a particularly effective dressing, especially when fished in a small ripple, but it will work even in calm conditions. It was first tied for Lough Corrib by Jack Ringrose of Kildysart, Co. Clare.

Rough Olive

PLATE 10

Hook: Size 12-14 Kamasan B175
Tying silk: Olive
Rib: Gold wire

Tail: Fibres of medium olive cock hackle
Body: Heron herl dyed olive
Hackle: Medium olive cock
Wing: Starling

A popular early-season river pattern for the top dropper. It is one of my favourites and it also has its uses on the lough when lake olives or olive buzzers are about.

Shipman's Buzzer

PLATE 11

Hook: Size 10-12 Kamasan B170
Tying silk: Black
Rib: Fine oval gold or silver tinsel or wire
Tail and head filaments: White polypropylene yarn
Body: Seal's fur

It is hard to decide whether these buzzers (invented by Dave Shipman) are wet or dry flies. They are fished 'damp' in the surface film of the lough when buzzers are hatching. Everyone has their own favourite body shade, depending on the colour of the emerging insect. Orange, olive, ginger, claret and black are most popular. Sometimes different colours of seal's fur are mixed, as in the case of the fly in the photograph, which is tied with natural seal's fur with a small pinch of hot orange mixed through it.

When the fly is tied, it is then roughed up well with a Velcro brush. It is preferable to use a Velcro brush instead of a dubbing needle as the body material should be 'roughed up' rather than picked out. Fish these flies static on a fine greased leader.

Silver Badger (trout)

PLATE 11

Hook: Size 8-10 Kamasan code M100
Tying silk: Black

Rib: Fine oval silver
Tail: Golden pheasant topping
Body: Flat silver
Hackle: Kingfisher blue cock
Wing: Badger hair

This fly appears to have originated on Lough Beltra, where it is used for grilse and seatrout. It is also fished on the Newport River (Co. Mayo) in the summer months and is especially attractive to fresh seatrout.

Silver Dabbler (Stuart McTeare)

PLATE 11

Hook: Size 8-10 Partridge stronghold
Tying silk: Black
Rib: Silver wire (to tie in palmered hackle)
Tail: Bronze mallard
Body: Claret seal's fur, ribbed with wide silver tinsel and well picked out
Hackle: Ginger hackle palmered, with another wound at shoulder
Wing: Bronze mallard tied all round
Head: Black silk, built up

Another fly in the Dabbler series, it is especially effective from midsummer when trout are likely to feed on fry. Fish it on the bob or on the point. It has caught many large trout for the originator, Stuart McTeare, on Lough Sheelin, including the Sheelin fly-caught record trout of 11lb 7oz, in 1994.

Silver Daddy

PLATE 11

Hook: Size 10 Partridge L2A
Tying silk: Black
Rib: Fine oval silver tinsel
Tail: Cock pheasant tail fibres, knotted two at a time and tied in $1/4$ inch above the knot, ten fibres in all

PLATE 11: WET FLIES
Top Row Shipman's Buzzer, Silver Daddy, Silver Badger (trout)
1st Row Silver Doctor (trout), Silver Dabbler (McTeare) Silver Invicta
2nd Row Silver March Brown, Silver Sedge, Small Yellow Mayfly, Silver Spider
3rd Row Soldier Palmer, Snipe & Orange, Snipe & Purple, Snipe & Yellow, Sooty Bumble
Bottom Row Sooty Olive, Stick Fly, Sooty Nymph, Sweeney Todd

Body: Flat silver tinsel
Legs: Cock pheasant centre tail fibres, knotted as for tail, twelve in all, and tied in $1/2$ inch from the knot. Three bunches are tied on top of the hook and three underneath
Hackle: Red-brown cock

The origins of the Silver Daddy are on Lough Corrib and the Connemara seatrout loughs. It is highly regarded as a seatrout fly, though it will take grilse too. It is best fished on the point. Those who use it describe it as being very good and well worth its place in August for wild brown trout. It should be tied with lots of legs.

Silver Doctor (trout)

PLATE 11

Hook: Size 8-12 Partridge L2A
Tying silk: Black
Tag: Fine oval silver - two turns
Tail: Golden pheasant topping
Butt: Red wool
Rib: Fine oval silver
Body: Flat silver
Hackle: Cambridge blue dyed cock (kingfisher will do)
Wing: Bronze mallard
Head: Red varnish

I first tied this fly for seatrout at Ballinahinch in 1981, at the request of Michael Conneely, the fishery manager. Since then it has become the first choice for night fishing at Ballynahinch. I have found it equally good for night fishing elsewhere in the west, for both river and lough. I find it most effective tied on a size 10 hook and fished on the top dropper on a floating line.

Fish it down and across on streamy water or with a slow figure-of-eight retrieve on slow pools or even from a boat at night on a lough (eg. Finlough at Delphi).

Silver Invicta

PLATE 11

Hook: Size 8-12 Partridge L2A
Tying silk: Black
Rib: Fine oval silver tinsel
Tail: Golden pheasant topping
Body: Flat silver tinsel
Hackle: Red game cock, palmered
Throat: Blue jay
Wing: Slips of hen pheasant centre tail or secondary wing quill

I have found the Silver Invicta a great all-round fly for browns, rainbows and seatrout. It is especially good when trout are taking perch fry, in which case it can be fished in the middle or on the point. It works well for rainbows, fished on a sinking line, and it is useful for seatrout on the lough and for grilse on the Erriff in low water.

Silver March Brown

PLATE 11

Hook: Size 10-12 Partridge L2A
Tying silk: Black or brown
Rib: Fine oval silver tinsel
Tail: Brown partridge fibres
Body: Flat silver tinsel
Hackle: Brown partridge
Wing: Hen pheasant secondary or slips of partridge tail

This fly is a variation of the March Brown. It is a useful fly in its own right, especially for brown trout or seatrout on the lough. Fish it when small sedges are about. Some regard it as a fly to be fished as a last hope when nothing else will work.

Silver Sedge

PLATE 11

Hook: Size 12-14 Partridge L2A

Tying silk: Grey or black
Rib: Fine oval silver or silver wire
Body: Grey seal's fur or grey floss silk
Hackle: Light ginger palmered and clipped on top
Wing: Slips of grey mallard wing quill tied sedge style
Head hackle: Light ginger cock

A fly to be fished either wet or dry when small light-coloured sedges are about, in the summer months, on either lough or river.

Silver Spider

PLATE 11

Hook: Size 12-16 Kamasan code M100
Tying silk: Black
Body: Flat silver tinsel
Rib (optional): Fine silver wire
Hackle: Two turns (maximum) of natural black hen

This is one of the best early-season wet-fly river patterns that I know for clear water. I prefer to fish it on the point but it works well too on the middle dropper. It also works well on the river in September. Its alternative use is for when duckfly are hatching in the evening.

Small Yellow Mayfly

PLATE 11

Hook: Size 12 Kamasan code M100
Tying silk: Brown
Rib: Fine oval gold tinsel
Tail: Three fibres of cock pheasant centre tail, tied short
Body: Lemon yellow seal's fur
Hackle: Lemon yellow cock with a small mallard drake breast feather dyed lemon yellow and tied in front. The mallard hackle is doubled before tying in

A great little Mayfly pattern to fish on the point, especially on Lough Conn. The dressing was given to me by Noel Ross of Dublin.

Soldier Palmer

PLATE 11

Hook: Size 10-12 Partridge L2A
Tying silk: Black
Rib: Fine oval gold tinsel
Tail: Red wool
Body: Red wool or seal's fur
Hackle: Red-brown cock palmered with a second hackle wound in front

A pattern for the loughs. It is probably taken by trout for an emerging sedge. Fish it on the top dropper and dibble it. There are several variations given for the dressing, but I prefer the one above.

Sooty Bumble (Christy Sleator)

PLATE 11

Hook: Size 10-12 Kamasan B175
Tying silk: Brown
Tag: Flat gold tinsel
Rib: Fine oval gold tinsel
Body: Dark olive seal's fur
Hackle: Dark olive cock palmered and a second one wound at the head

A pattern devised for Lough Ennell by that master lough fisher Christy Sleator of Mullingar. It is an excellent fly for the top dropper when lake olives are hatching, but it is also a good all-round pattern and can be equally effective when fished on the point.

Snipe & Purple

PLATE 11

Hook: Size 12-16 Kamasan B160

Tying silk: Purple
Body: Tying silk
Hackle: Dark snipe tied sparsely

An excellent early-season pattern for the river, especially when iron blue duns are hatching.

Small Dark Olive Nymph

The same tying will do as for the Medium Olive Nymph, p43.

Snipe & Orange

PLATE 11

Hook: Size 12-14 Kamasan B160
Tying silk: Orange
Rib: Gold wire
Body: Orange floss
Hackle: Snipe

A fly for the river. Fish it on the point. It is said that trout take it for a shrimp.

Snipe & Yellow

PLATE 11

Hook: Size 12-14 Kamasan B160
Tying silk: Yellow
Body: Tying silk
Hackle: Dark snipe tied sparsely

A useful fly on the river when pale wateries or light olives are hatching.

Sooty Olive

PLATE 11

Hook: Size 8-14 Kamasan B175
Tying silk: Black or brown
Rib: Fine oval gold tinsel
Tail: Golden pheasant tippets
Body: Dark olive and brown olive seal's fur mixed in equal parts

Hackle: Natural black hen
Wing: Bronze mallard

The Sooty Olive is the quintessential Irish lough fly. In different sizes and different positions on the leader it could usefully be fished all season. Its origins are probably lost, though I suspect it is a Rogan pattern. It is hard to say what is the standard dressing, but the one given above works well for me. The hackle is black cock, but on the western loughs a sooty olive hackle is preferred. This shade is obtained by dying a red game cock cape, dark olive, using Veniard's dark olive dye.

This is a good general-purpose pattern. It is especially effective in size 12 when duckflies are hatching. Cast it into the rings of a rising trout and don't move it. Alternatively, it can be fished on the point, where it may be taken for a shrimp. It is also useful when olive buzzers or lake olives are hatching. Finally, it makes a useful river fly in spring, in small sizes.

Stick Fly

PLATE 11

Hook: Size 8-10 Kamasan B830
Tying silk: Yellow
Rib: Copper wire
Underbody: A few turns of fine lead wire - or copper wire
Body: Bronze peacock herl
Hackle: A couple of turns of ginger hen
Head: Yellow wool

The Stick Fly is a good imitation of the larva of the caddis or sedge fly. I find this an especially useful pattern for the river, fished on the point, early in the season. It has its uses on the lough about the same time. Different dressings are given, but the one above is simple and works for me. It is not always necessary to wind an underbody. Sometimes a yellow or fluorescent green wool tail is used, in which case omit the yellow head and tie in the hackle at the end.

Sweeney Todd

PLATE 11

Hook: Size 6-12 Kamasan B830
Tying silk: Black
Rib: Flat silver tinsel
Body: Black floss
Thorax or front quarter of body: Neon magenta DFM wool or floss
Hackle: Crimson cock hackle tied in as beard at the throat
Wing: Black squirrel

The usefulness of this fly (from Richard Walker and Peter Thomas) is not just confined to reservoirs. I find it to be one of the most useful early-season lough patterns for brown trout. I fish it on the point in shallow water in March and April.

Sooty Nymph

PLATE 11

Hook: Size 12-14 Kamasan B160
Tying silk: Black
Tag: Three turns oval gold tinsel tied round the bend
Rib: Fine oval gold tinsel.
Body: Dark olive and brown olive seal's fur mixed in equal parts
Hackle: Short natural black hen tied sparsely
Eyes: Small jungle cock

A nymph for when buzzers are hatching and trout are moving to them in a small ripple.

Teal & Black

PLATE 12

Hook: Size 10-14 Kamasan B175
Tying silk: Black
Rib: Silver wire
Body: Black floss
Hackle: Black hen
Wing: Teal flank

A good fly in a wave when duckflies or black buzzers are hatching. Fish it on the top dropper, where it seems to me it gives much better results in the smaller sizes if fished on a sinking line. It is useful again late in the season when small black midges are about on the lough.

Teal Blue & Silver

PLATE 12

Hook: Size 8-14 Kamasan code M100
Tying silk: Black
Rib: Fine oval silver tinsel
Tail: Golden pheasant tippets
Body: Flat silver tinsel
Hackle: Cock dyed kingfisher or teal blue
Wing: Teal flank

The Teal Blue & Silver is primarily regarded as a seatrout fly for the west and south, where it is fished on both lough and river. It is a good daytime choice on the lough, especially for fresh-run trout, and will take finnock well, in September.

Teal & Yellow

PLATE 12

Hook: Size 8-14 Kamasan code M100
Tying silk: Yellow or brown
Rib: Fine oval silver
Tail: Golden pheasant tippets
Body: Yellow seal's fur
Hackle: Ginger cock
Wing: Teal flank

Another of the Teal series. Some like to fish it on the dropper on the lough in a mayfly hatch. In that position it is a good option during the mayfly hatch that occurs in late

July and early August on some lakes.

Ted's Special

PLATE 12

Hook: Size 4-8 longshank
Tying silk: Black
Rib: Fine oval silver
Body: Rear two-thirds, flat silver tinsel;
front third, red floss silk or red wool
Wing: Long bronze and/or grey mallard
flank, extending well beyond the bend of the
hook and secured at the head and at the end
of the body
Gill pads: Jungle cock
Head: Well built up with the tying silk, and
an underlay of lead wire, varnished black
and an eye painted with white and black
varnish.

For those who like to fish a lure to rising
trout, this is the one. It is not often that one
comes across a fly that gets such a quick
response when cast across the path of a
feeding fish. It is best used on a sinking line
or shooting head and stripped fast. Be
prepared for very aggressive takes! The
invention of the late Ted McKee of Lisburn,
this fly was known only to a small number of
anglers for years. It has caught thousands of
lough and reservoir trout in its time.

Thunder & Lightning (trout)

PLATE 12

Hook: Size 8-12 Kamasan code M100
Tying silk: Black
Rib: Fine oval gold tinsel
Tail: Golden pheasant topping
Body: Black floss silk
Hackle: Orange cock (sometimes palmered)
with blue jay at the throat
Wing: Bronze mallard
Eyes: Jungle cock

This is the seatrout version of the old Irish
salmon pattern of the same name. It is
mainly fished on the loughs from July to
September, where it will also take summer
salmon. It can be fished in any position on
the leader but I prefer it on the bob last
thing in the evening.

Water Boatman

See Corixa

Watson's Bumble

PLATE 12

Hook: Size 8-14, Partridge L2A or Kamasan
M100
Tying silk: Black
Rib: Fine oval or flat silver tinsel
Tail: Golden pheasant topping
Body: Rear half, red seal's fur; front half,
black seal's fur
Hackle: Black cock palmered with three or
four turns of blue jay wound in front
Eyes: Jungle cock

It is often a tribute to the effectiveness of a
fly when it begets variants. This close
relative of the Watson's Fancy (below) is
especially well thought of on Lough
Currane, where it is rated as highly by some
as the Bibio or the Claret Bumble as a top-
dropper fly for seatrout.

Watson's Fancy

PLATE 12

Hook: Size 8-14, Partridge L2A or Kamasan
M100
Tying silk: Black
Rib: Fine oval silver tinsel
Tail: Golden pheasant topping
Body: Rear half, red seal's fur; front half,
black seal's fur
Hackle: Black cock
Wing: Slips of crow wing

Eyes: Jungle cock.

This traditional Scottish pattern is a big favourite in Ireland and you will scarcely ever find it missing from the fly box of either a seatrout fisher or a brown trout lough fisher. Fish it in small sizes when duckfly are hatching. Later in August and September it is a good fly on the point or dropper in size 10 and 12. It is an excellent late-season seatrout fly and if there are grilse in a lough they will take it too. I like to tie it with a black squirrel wing for grilse.

Welshman's Button Pupa

PLATE 12

Hook: Size 10 Partridge GRS6A or Yorkshire sedge hook
Tying silk: Yellow
Rib: Flat gold tinsel
Back: Slip of dark turkey, 1/2 inch wide
Body: Yellow and pale olive seal's fur mixed in equal parts
Wings: Slips of woodcock wing quill tied in short to lie along the body
Legs: A pinch of bronze mallard tied in as a false hackle and extending past bend of hook

When the Welshman's button sedge emerges on lakes in late May and early June the trout frequently shun the adult fly in favour of the pupa. This is especially true on Lough Ennell. In such situations it is important to have a pupa pattern to hand and the above dressing is one option.

White Hackle Invicta

PLATE 12

Hook: Size 10-12 Kamasan B175
Tying silk: Brown
Rib: Fine oval gold tinsel
Tail: Golden pheasant topping

Body: Yellow seal's fur
Hackle: Ginger cock, palmered
Wing: Hen pheasant secondary
Front hackle: White cock, long in fibre, wound full circle

The Invicta can be a useful fly at mayfly time, fished on the point or middle dropper. However, those who use the White Hackle Invicta on Lough Conn claim that when tied on a size 12 hook and fished on the top dropper it will outfish the standard pattern at least four to one.

Wickham's Fancy

PLATE 12

Hook: Size 8-14 Kamasan B175
Tying silk: Brown
Rib: Fine oval gold tinsel
Tail: Fibres of ginger red hackle
Body: Flat gold tinsel
Hackle: Ginger-red cock hackle, palmered
Wing: Slips of grey duck wing quill

This is a pattern for brown trout on the loughs. It is generally regarded as a good top-dropper fly in the summer when sedges are about. However, I have also found it to be an excellent attractor fly, fished on the point in fairly shallow water on a bright sunny day, when there is no fly about on the surface. It works well in this situation in early May on Lough Corrib.

Williams Favourite

PLATE 12

Hook: Size 12-14 Kamasan B175
Tying silk: Black
Rib: Silver wire
Tail: Black cock hackle fibres
Body: Black floss
Hackle: Black hen tied sparsely

This is a useful fly on the river in May, June

and September. Fish it on the point. It is also an excellent fly when black buzzers or midges are returning to the water. Fish it on a fine leader, static, in flat calm or a small ripple or cast it in the path of feeding trout. I sometimes omit the tail in this situation. A Williams Favourite and a Millerman make an ideal team.

Willie's Fancy

PLATE 12

Hook: Size 8-12 Kamasan B170
Tying silk: Black
Body: Pearl Mylar tubing
Hackle: Dyed red cock, tied as beard hackle
Wing: White bucktail under green bucktail
Head: Black with a white Tippex eye

This fly was first brought to my attention by Willie McAndrew of Castlebar when we were fishing for seatrout on the Moy estuary. The name Willie's Fancy may not be right, but as a taker of seatrout in brackish water it has few equals. Fish it on the dropper on a sinking line and strip it fast.

Woodcock & Yellow

PLATE 12

Hook: Size 12 Kamasan B175
Tying silk: Olive
Rib: Fine oval gold tinsel
Tail: Golden pheasant tippets
Body: Yellow seal's fur
Hackle: Yellow hen
Wing: Slips of woodcock wing

Michael Kennedy describes this fly as being of proven merit and it can bring success when buzzers or sedges are hatching.

Yellow Mayfly (Michael Kelly)

PLATE 12

Hook: Size 8-10 Partridge L2A

Tying silk: Brown
Rib: Fine oval gold tinsel
Tail: Fibres of cock pheasant tail
Body: Pale olive seal's fur
Hackle: Dyed red cock with a dyed lemon yellow mallard flank feather doubled and wound in front

A pattern that takes a lot of trout on Lough Mask. It was first tied by Michael Kelly of Balbriggan.

Yellow Tip (Billy Quail)

PLATE 12

Hook: Size 12-14 Kamasan B160
Tying silk: Black
Rib: Fine copper wire
Tag: DFM yellow floss
Body: Fibres of cock pheasant centre tail
Hackle: Two turns of Greenwell's hen

This is a pattern for small lakes. It gives best results - and they can be very good - when fished in the surface film when trout are feeding on daphnia, as dusk approaches on summer evenings.

Zulu

PLATE 12

Hook: Size 8-14 Kamasan B175
Tying silk: Black
Rib: Fine oval silver tinsel
Tail: Red wool
Body: Black seal's fur
Hackle: Black cock palmered, with a second black hackle wound in front

The Zulu is generally used as a top-dropper fly on the lough where it will take both brown trout and seatrout. I have found it especially effective in September for trout feeding on corixa in shallow water and close to the shore.

PLATE 12: WET FLIES
Top Row Teal & Black, Teal Blue & Silver, Teal & Yellow, Thunder & Lightning (trout)
1st Row Welshman's Button Pupa, Ted's Special, Watson's Fancy
2nd Row White Hackle Invicta, Watson's Bumble, Williams Favourite, Wickham's Fancy
3rd Row Woodcock & Yellow, Yellow Tip, Willie's Fancy
Bottom Row Yellow Mayfly (Kelly), Zulu

The Dry Flies

━━━━━━━

In Ireland, dry fly fishing is mainly practised on the rivers, for brown trout. There is, however, a sizeable group of anglers who use dry flies in certain situations on the loughs, and even seatrout can be tempted from time to time with a dry fly on either river or lough.

Fishing the dry fly calls for a fairly high degree of casting skill. The fly must be presented accurately and gently. It must, on occasions, be carefully chosen too, to match the natural fly that the trout is feeding on at the time. At other times a well presented general pattern may do just as well.

My earliest memories of flyfishing are of dry fly anglers at mayfly time on the river Annalee. If, in those far off, post-war days of scarce flytying materials and inferior tackle, these anglers were able to muster the bare necessities of tackle and flies and master the skill to present the fly appetizingly, then the anglers of today have little excuse when one considers the sheer range of materials, tackle and information that is now so readily available.

The dry fly tradition is still very strong on the rivers. River fishers, especially in the summer months, will find that the dry fly brings with it a lot of opportunities and a great deal of fun.

It would be a mistake to conclude that dry fly fishing in Ireland is confined only to rivers. It has a long history of use on the loughs too, especially in the Midlands. When trout move around, close to the surface sipping down flies, the angler would be well advised to get out a dry fly and cast it in the path of the feeding fish. Dry fly fishing opportunities occur on the loughs mainly at buzzer time, mayfly time and sedge time, but there will be other opportunities as well.

The dry flies included here are intended to provide the angler with a comprehensive range of artificials to cope with the principal fly hatches that occur throughout the season, on both river and lough.

Adams

PLATE 13

Hook: Size 14-18, Partridge L3A
Tying silk: Grey or black
Tail: Mixed grizzle and red-brown cock hackle fibres
Body: Musk-rat fur
Wing: Two grizzle hackle tips
Hackle: A grizzle hackle and a red-brown hackle wound through each other

This is an excellent nondescript pattern for use when in doubt as to what to try next! It is one of North America's most popular patterns and it will work here, especially early in the season on the poorer upland streams, even when naturals are not hatching.
Also effective during olive hatches early in the season or when trout are taking the adult buzzers.

Alder

PLATE 13

Hook: Size 10-12, Partridge L3A
Tying silk: Black
Body: Peacock herl, dyed magenta
Wing: Brown speckled hen quill tied low, sedge style, over body
Hackle: Black cock

The alder looks a bit like a dark sedge. It is a terrestrial fly that hatches in May and early June. It is a weak flier and it often gets blown on to rivers and loughs.

Amber Spinner

PLATE 13

Hook: Size 12-14
Tying silk: Orange
Rib: Orange tying silk
Tail: Fibres of honey hackle
Body: Amber seal's fur substitute
Hackle: Six turns of cree cock with upper and lower fibres cut away or tied figure-of-eight

A pattern for summer evenings when the spinners of pale wateries are on the water.

Amber Spinner (T. Clegg)

PLATE 13

Hook: Size 14-16, Kamasan B160
Tying silk: Primrose
Wings: Lengths of electron white DRF floss, tied spent and equally divided
Rib: Brown Naples silk
Tail: Cock fibres dyed slate-grey
Body: Arc Chrome DRF floss
Hackle: Slate-grey cock

A successful pattern for mid-summer when rivers are running low and very clear.

Ant

PLATE 13

Hook: Size 14, Kamasan B160
Tying silk: Brown
Body: Short length of Ethafoam, dyed brown with waterproof pen, trimmed with scissors and secured by the middle at the mid-point

PLATE 13: DRY FLIES

Top Row Adams, Apple Green Buzzer, Autumn Dun
1st Row Amber Spinner, Alder, Amber Spinner (Clegg)
2nd Row Black Gnat (Weaver), Ant, Black Midge (Parry)
Bottom Row Badger Quill, Balling Buzzer, Beacon Beige (Deane)

of the hook shank
Hackle: Red game cock, wound at the middle of the body

Ants come in several colours but brown seems to be the most common. They take to the wing in late July and August, when conditions are right - usually warm humid days and evenings - and get blown on to the rivers and loughs where they bring on frantic rises of both brown trout and seatrout. At such times it is imperative to have an artificial imitation to hand.

Apple Green Buzzer

PLATE 13

Hook: Size 14-16, Partridge CS20
Tying silk: Primrose
Tail: A few whisks of white hackle fibres
Rib: Fine gold wire
Body: Gütermann's sewing thread - shade 616 - is preferred. An alternative is pale olive dubbing or the fine flue from the base of a pale olive dyed hackle
Hackle: Cream cock hackle or cream-tipped badger cock hackle

The apple-green buzzer (*Endochironomus albipennis*) hatches during the day and early evening on certain loughs during the summer months. This is a small fly, easily recognised by its bright green body. If the hatch is plentiful, trout will occasionally feed on the adult flies along the edge of a ripple, in quiet bays and in areas of calm water.

Autumn Dun

PLATE 13

Hook: Size 14-16
Tying silk: Olive
Rib: Gold wire
Tail: Fibres of red-brown hackle

Body: Olive-green seal's fur and hare's body fur mixed
Hackle: A grizzle cock hackle and a pale olive hackle wound through each other

Autumn duns (*Ecdyonurus dispar*) and the large green duns (*Ecdyonurus insignis*) usually occur on the stony stretches of moorland rivers from early May onwards. They can bring on a good rise of trout during the summer and the above dressing should enable you to cope in this situation. When the spinners return to the water, try fishing a Pheasant Tail Spinner.

Badger Quill

PLATE 13

Hook: Size 14-16, Kamasan B170
Tying silk: Primrose
Tail: Fibres of badger cock hackle
Body: Stripped peacock eye quill
Hackle: Badger cock

The Badger Quill is a good general spinner pattern and this dressing will also tempt trout taking pale wateries.

Balling Buzzer

PLATE 13

Hook: Size 8-10, Kamasan B170 or B830
Tying silk: Black
Body: None
Rib: A series of badger and grizzle cock hackles, long in fibre, palmered alternately up the full length of the hook shank

On warm summer days on the limestone loughs in June and early July, mating buzzers sometimes form themselves into clumps as big as golf balls and literally roll along the surface. They provide tasty mouthfuls for big trout and on such occasions a well-oiled Balling Buzzer is called for.

Beacon Beige *(Peter Deane)*

PLATE 13

Hook: Size 14-16, Partridge L3A or Kamasan B170
Tying silk: Black
Tail: Fibres of grizzle cock hackle
Body: Stripped peacock eye quill
Hackle: Grizzle cock and red game wound through each other

This Peter Deane pattern is one of my favourite river flies and my fly box is always well stocked with a range of sizes. It is a useful olive imitation and will even pull up a trout when no flies are hatching.

Black Gnat *(Mike Weaver)*

PLATE 13

Hook: Size 16-22, Partridge CS20
Tying silk: Black or grey
Body: Fine black fur
Wing: White poly yarn
Hackle: Black cock

There are many good black gnat imitations and Mike Weaver's is one such. This fly (*Bibio johannis*) is a terrestrial. It can be seen in swarms close to the ground or over water in warm sultry weather and it falls in big numbers on rivers and in quiet corners on the edge of loughs from June to September. When fishing for trout taking black gnat on dead pools, never cast directly to the trout. Rather, observe how it patrols and then cast the fly to a point to which you know the trout will return - and wait! Trout will often take a simulium pattern (see Simulium, page 90) in this situation.

Black Midge *(Bill Percy)*

PLATE 13

Hook: Size 14-16, Kamasan B160

Tying silk: Black
Tag: Fine flat silver tinsel
Body: Bronze peacock herl
Hackle: Black cock

Anglers often refer to trout 'taking black midge' without being specific as to whether it is the black gnat of the previous dressing, or the reed smut (Simulium, page 90). Trout will generally take either a Black Gnat or a Simulium pattern, provided the size is right. This is an excellent tying by the late Bill Percy, of Lurgan, and one I use a lot.

Black Sedge

PLATE 14

Hook: Size 12-14, Partridge L3A
Tying silk: Black
Rib: Gold wire
Body: Black wool or black feather fibres (crow)
Wing: Dark speckled hen
Front hackle: Red-brown or coch-y-bondhu cock

This pattern will represent various black sedges, including the black silverhorn sedge. Sedge imitations are suggestive rather than exact imitations, since trout probably recognise a sedge more by its shape or silhouette rather than by the overall accuracy of its features.

Bluebottle *(Billy Quail)*

PLATE 14

Hook: Size 12-14, Kamasan B 170
Tying silk: Red
Rib: Narrow peacock herl
Body: Pale blue floss
Body hackle: Black cock, palmered
Wing: Two blue dun hackle points tied back over the body and divided
Front hackle: Black dyed cock hackle

This is a good imitation of the bluebottle or house fly, a terrestrial that often finds its way on to the water on sultry summer days. It is also a good fly for taking river trout when no flies are about in summer. Cast it into quiet pockets of deep water under overhanging bankside trees.

Blue Quill (Billy Quail)

PLATE 14

Hook: Size 14, Kamasan B170
Tying silk: Black
Tail: Pale blue dun cock
Body: Stripped peacock eye quill
Hackle: White tipped badger dyed pale blue dun

An early-season pattern for the river when medium olives (*Baetis tenax*) are about in April and May. They usually hatch around midday.

Blue-Winged Olive Dun (John Bradley)

PLATE 14

Hook: Size 16, Kamasan B175
Tying silk: Black
Tail: Three fibre points of cock pheasant (centre tail) tied short
Body: blue-wing olive Fly-Rite poly dubbing
Hackle: Dark blue dun cock

The blue-winged olive (*Ephemerella ignita*) is important from May to September, especially on rivers. From mid-June to mid-August, it hatches mainly in the evening; and by day for the remainder of its season. It is one of the most important of our upwinged river flies. The spinner is the sherry spinner. The artificial imitations are legion but I have found this pattern, tied by John Bradley of Navan, to be one of the best. Other proven patterns for Irish rivers are listed below.

Blue-Winged Olive (Michael Kennedy)

PLATE 14

Hook: Size 16, Kamasan B175
Tying silk: Olive
Rib: Fine gold wire
Tail: Fibres of ginger cock
Body: Yellow-olive seal's fur or other fine pale olive fur
Hackle: A couple of turns of (pale) yellow-olive cock with a dark blue dun cock wound in front

Dr Ken Whelan rates this pattern very highly for September BWO hatches. Other useful Blue-Winged Olive patterns are the Orange Quill, Mike Weaver's Orange Sparkle Dun and Peter Brown's Blue-Winged Olive.

Blue-Winged Olive (Peter Brown)

PLATE 14

Hook: Size 16-18, Partridge L3A
Tying silk: Primrose
Tail: Light blue dun cock hackle fibres
Body: Yellow silk
Hackle: A blue-grey dyed cock hackle or blue dun

The hackle of this fly has a distinct smoky-grey appearance.

Brown Flag

PLATE 14

Hook: Size 12-14, Partridge L3A
Tying silk: Black
Rib: Gold wire
Body: Hare's ear
Body hackle: Coch-y-bondhu cock

Plate 14: Dry Flies

Top Row Black Sedge, Bluebottle (Quail), Blue Quill (Quail)
1st Row Blue-Winged Olive (Kennedy), Blue-Winged Olive Dun (Bradley),
Blue-Winged Olive (Brown)
2nd Row Brown Olive (Quail), Brown Flag, Caenis
Bottom Row Campto Chironomid, Caperer, Claret Dun (Harris)

Wing: Brown speckled hen wing quill
Front hackle: Red-brown cock hackle

This dressing is a slight variation of Dr Michael Kennedy's excellent dressing for the brown flag (*Hydropsyche ornatula*) which occurs on limestone rivers between mid-May and mid-June. It will also take trout when various brown sedges are about. When tying, clip the body hackle short on top.

Brown Olive (Billy Quail)

Plate 14

Hook: Size 14, Partridge L3A or Kamasan B170
Tying silk: Black
Tail: Fibres of brown-olive dyed hackle
Body: Stripped peacock eye quill
Hackle: Brown-olive cock (a ginger or honey hackle dyed brown-olive)

A pattern for March, April and early May when trout are taking large dark olives (*Baetis rhodani*) on the river.

Caenis

Plate 14

Hook: Size 14-16, Kamasan B160
Tying silk: Brown
Tail: White hackle fibres
Body: Natural seal's fur
Hackle: A couple of turns of white cock with black cock wound in front

Caenis hatch at dawn and dusk in late June, July and early August. Trout taking them are difficult to catch, especially in the evening, but I have found the above dressing successful in the early morning on the lough. Find a calm corner by the shore or in the shelter of an island and fish from the shore casting this fly on a fine leader in the path of the feeding trout. I have also found a small Grey Duster to work in this situation.

Campto Chironomid

Plate 14

Hook: Size 12, Kamasan B175
Tying silk: Black
Body: Stripped peacock eye quill tied partly around the bend
Wing: Starling
Hackle: A badger cock and a Greenwell cock hackle wound together
Head: DFM green wool

The campto buzzer emerges on certain loughs between May and August. It is a large buzzer and a distinguishing feature is its striped yellow and black head. Trout love it and will take it especially well early in the morning and just before dusk.

I first tied the above pattern in about 1980 and it works well when trout are taking the emerging fly or when females are returning to the water. I have also found it to work for trout taking caenis as darkness closes in.

Caperer

Plate 14

Hook: Size 10-12, Partridge L3A
Tying silk: Orange
Rib: Gold wire
Body: Pale olive seal's fur
Body hackle: Ginger
Wing: Speckled light brown or cinnamon hen
Hackle: Ginger

The caperer (*Halesus spp*) is a sedge that hatches on loughs between July and October and emerges in open water. This pattern is best fished with a slow figure-of-eight retrieve, pausing occasionally. It can also be fished as a top dropper fly. This pattern will also suffice for the cinnamon sedge.

Claret Dun (J.R.Harris)

PLATE 14

Hook: Size 14-16, Partridge L3A
Tying silk: Claret
Rib: Fine gold wire
Tail: Fibres of dark blue dun cock hackle
Body: Heron substitute dyed claret, or mole's fur and dark claret mohair mixed
Hackle: Dark blue dun cock

The claret dun (*Leptophlebia vespertina*) occurs mainly in moorland loughs, on the sluggish stretches of moorland rivers and on the bog bays of limestone loughs. It hatches between April and the end of July during the day and is especially prevalent on the moorland and mountain loughs.

Coachman

PLATE 15

Hook: Size 14, Kamasan B160
Tying silk: Black
Body: Peacock herl
Wings: Two white hackle tips tied upright and divided
Hackle: Red-brown cock

A good general pattern in fading light on summer evenings on the river.

Copydex Spent Gnat (Barrie Cooke)

PLATE 15

Hook: Size 12-14, Partridge B2A wee double
Tying silk: Brown
Tail: Four fibres of cock pheasant centre tail
Body: Copydex adhesive (see below)
Hackle: A creamy-white cock hackle wound behind a black cock hackle and the two then divided with figure-of-eight turns of the silk and tied spent fashion, or it may be dressed

as a half-spent pattern

The Copydex Spent Gnat is an amazingly realistic and effective pattern. It is the creation of artist Barrie Cooke for Lough Arrow and was popularised by the TV programme and video *The Irish Mayfly* by David Shaw-Smith.

To make the body, take a sheet of glass or a mirror and spread a thin film of Copydex, about one inch wide and 4 inches long. Allow it to dry. When dry, make two strokes, lengthwise, with a brown waterproof pen near one side of the Copydex film. This will simulate the brown markings on the natural fly.

Now take the four fibres of cock pheasant tail, cut to length, and place the cut ends at the side and towards one end of the film. With the fingers, gently begin rolling the Copydex and encircle the ends of the pheasant tail fibres. Continue rolling the body till all of the clear film is formed into a long, thin, flexible cylinder about the thickness of a match. Tie this on to the hook shank about quarter way back from the eye.

Cul de Canard (Andrew Ryan)

PLATE 15

Hook: Size 14-16, Kamasan B160
Tying silk: Black
Tail: Fibres of dark dun cock hackle
Body: Blue-grey rabbit fur
Hackle: A cul de canard feather wound at the head and then clipped

Cul de canard feathers - the oily feathers from the mallard's preen gland - have a multitude of uses for dry flies and emergers. This one, which Andrew Ryan calls his Cul de Canard, is very effective as a fishing-the-water-fly, especially on fast glides. It will take trout when there is a hatch of olives and also when midges are about. It is possible to change the body colour to match the hatch, but keep the same basic hackle style. When the hackle is wound, draw the fibres forward over the eye of the hook and clip off the ends to the required length.

Cul de Canard Sedge

PLATE 15

Hook: Size 14-16, Kamasan B170
Tying silk: Black
Body: Grey ostrich herl clipped short
Wing: A bunch of cul de canard feathers tied in at the head and clipped short above the hook bend
Hackle: Grizzle cock

A dressing from the River Suir. This is a great little sedge imitation, being very visible and therefore especially good at night.

Daddy

PLATE 15

Hook: Size 8-10, Kamasan B170
Tying silk: Black
Rib: Fine oval gold tinsel
Body: Natural raffia
Wings: Badger cock hackle points tied spent
Legs: Six cock pheasant centre tail fibres knotted, four tied to lie backwards and two to lie forwards
Hackle: Red game cock

When daddies are about in the month of August they often get blown on to the water. Their tumbling, ungainly passage across the water will soon tempt up even the most taciturn of fish.

A good floating artificial will then be called for as brown trout, seatrout - sometimes even salmon - decide to take the naturals from the surface of lough or river.

Dark Midge (Andrew Ryan)

PLATE 15

Hook: Size 12-16, Kamasan B160
Tying silk: Black
Tail: Fibres of dark blue dun hackle
Body: Blue rabbit underfur
Hackle: Dark blue dun cock

Few anglers recognise how important small midge (*Chironomus spp*) patterns can be on the river, even by day, all through the summer months. If in doubt, ask a trout! It will also confirm that when it wants a dark pattern a light one just will not do, and *vice versa*.

Dark Olive

See Large Dark Olive, page 80; or Small Dark Olive, page 90.

Devaux Sedge

PLATE 15

Hook: Size 10-12, Kamasan B170
Tying silk: Black
Wing: Three feathers from the flank or breast of a mallard duck, varnished and trimmed to shape
Hackle: Ginger cock

I don't know of a better sedge pattern for river fishing than this one. The colour can be altered by using different coloured feathers for the wing, e.g. use brown mallard drake neck feathers to get a brown sedge and the hackle can be varied from grizzle through to red brown cock.

A note on tying. The fly has no body. To prepare the breast or flank feathers strip away the waste at the base. Then tie them one at a time, on top of each other and soak with Floo Gloo or with clear varnish, applying it with finger and thumb and stroking backwards. As the varnish dries, the

PLATE 15: DRY FLIES

Top Row Coachman, Cul de Carnard (Ryan), Dark Midge (Ryan)
1st Row Dry Buzzer, Copydex Spent Gnat (Ryan), Cul de Canard Sedge
2nd Row Daddy, Devaux Sedge
Bottom Row Ethafoam Sedge, Fanwing Mayfly

feathers will stick together to give a unique sedge profile. Trim with sharp scissors, if the wing is considered too long.

Dry Buzzer

PLATE 15

Hook: Size 12-14, Kamasan B170
Tying silk: Black
Rib: Gold wire
Body: Dark olive seal's fur
Hackle: White-tipped badger cock

When buzzers return to the water to lay their eggs, it often coincides with a hatch of another generation of the same fly. If they are plentiful on the lough surface trout will feed on the newly-hatched adult fly in the evening and at dusk in early and mid-summer. This pattern is fished dry and stationary and has proved its worth.

Ethafoam Sedge

PLATE 15

Hook: Size 12-14 sedge hook
Tying silk: Black
Body and head: Lemon-yellow Ethafoam
Wing: Sika deerhair

This is a superb hatching sedge pattern for river trout. In Ireland it is best known on the Suir although it is attributed to the Austrian flytyer, Roman Moser.

Tying tips. Place the hook in the vice and take the silk to the end of the hook shank. Then take a $^1/_2$cm-square length of lemon-yellow Ethafoam and bind down on top of the hook shank with open turns of tying silk leaving the end of the Ethafoam extending out over the hook eye. Now tie in the wing and double the Ethafoam back over the wing butt, secure it with a couple of turns of silk and then tie off.

Fanwing Mayfly

PLATE 15

Hook: Size 8-10, Kamasan B170 or B830
Tying silk: Brown
Body: Natural raffia
Rib: Red floss tightly twisted
Tail: cock pheasant centre tail, 3 or 4 fibres
Wings: Two mallard drake breast feathers dyed lemon-yellow
Hackle: Light red game

This is a traditional west of Ireland pattern for Corrib, Mask, Conn and Carra. It can be fished dry and static or on the bob greased up with a team of wet flies.

Ginger Quill

PLATE 16

Hook: Size 14-16, Partridge L3A
Tying silk: Brown
Tail: Ginger cock hackle fibres
Body: Stripped peacock eye quill
Hackle: Ginger cock

A good general pattern for when olives are about, particularly medium olives (*Baetis tenax*), or the pale wateries. It will even take trout feeding on lake olives.

Gold-Ribbed Hare's Ear

PLATE 16

Hook: Size 14-16, Kamasan B170
Tying silk: Primrose
Rib: Gold wire
Tail: Guard hairs from a hare's mask
Body: Hare's ear
Hackle: Dark dun cock or ginger cock tied in a half-circle

A great little general pattern for small dark olives (*Baetis scambus*) in July and August, for medium olives (*Baetis tenax*) in May and

June and for the large dark olive (*Baetis rhodani*) earlier in the season.

Green Midge (Billy Quail)

PLATE 16

Hook: Size 14-16
Tying silk: Primrose
Body: Insect-green dyed goose herl
Body hackle: Close-clipped grizzle cock
Hackle: Grizzle

An excellent floating pattern to imitate the apple green midge (*E. albipennis*) on loughs in the summer months. It hatches during the day and while the trout are extremely fond of the pupa (see Apple Green Buzzer, page 2) they will also at the same time switch and take the adult fly. Since it is such a small pattern, it is best fished on a fine leader in calm water or close by the edge of a ripple, behind a promontory or on the sheltered side of an island.

Green Peter

PLATE 16

Hook: Size 6-8, Partridge L3A
Tying silk: Black
Rib: Fine oval gold tinsel
Body: Green-olive or dark olive seal's fur
Body hackle: Ginger cock clipped on top to allow the wing to lie flat
Wing: Oak speckled turkey tail
Hackle: Ginger or red game cock

When the big green peter (*Phryganea varia* and *P. obsoleta*) hatches take place at dusk on the Midland lakes in late July and early August, anglers are usually not the slightest bit concerned about which species is emerging or whether the body colour is olive or black. What is important is to have a good floating dressing approximately the same shade as the natural insect. This pattern fits the bill.

If speckled turkey is not available, use four slips from a long-fibred hen pheasant secondary quill. The wing must be tied on flat so as to envelop the top of the body, not allowing any light between wing and body.

Greenwell's Glory

PLATE 16

Hook: Size 12-16, Kamasan B170
Tying silk: Yellow silk pulled through brown cobbler's wax
Rib: Fine gold wire
Tail: Greenwell hackle fibres
Body: Waxed yellow tying silk (olive hue)
Hackle: Greenwell cock

This is a good general imitation pattern for many of the darker olives. It is especially useful for large dark olives and medium olives on the river and for the lake olive. A starling's wing is optional.

Greenwell's Parachute

PLATE 16

Hook: 12-14, Kamasan B170
Tying silk: Yellow silk pulled through brown cobbler's wax (brown)
Rib: Gold wire
Tail: Greenwell hackle fibres
Body: Tying silk
Wing: Starling
Hackle: Greenwell's cock tied in the parachute style.

Leslie Murray's most favoured dressing for fishing the hill loughs early in the season.

Grey Duster

PLATE 16

Hook: Size 12-16, Partridge L3A
Tying silk: Black

75

Body: Blue-grey rabbit fur
Hackle: Badger cock hackle

A great little dry fly for both river and lough. It is widely used at dusk on the loughs when trout are feeding on adult buzzers. It will also take trout feeding on caenis if fished in small sizes on a very fine leader in the flat calm. It also works for small grey midges on the river. In all these instances it should be dressed with a well marked white-tipped badger cock hackle. Try it even at mayfly time when the trout may be taking the pale watery duns (*C. luteolum*) and not the mayfly. In this situation a cream-tipped badger hackle will be more effective.

Grey Flag

PLATE 16

Hook: Size 12-14, Partridge L3A
Tying silk: Grey or black
Rib: Silver wire or fine silver tinsel
Body: Blue rabbit fur or grey heron herl
Body hackle: Badger cock
Wing: Hen pheasant secondary or woodcock wing slips
Front hackle: Badger cock

When the Grey flag (*Hydropsyche spp*) hatches on the rivers of the east coast (such as the Boyne and Liffey) in May and June, many anglers consider this pattern indispensable. When the hatch is at its peak the flies appear both during the day and at dusk, bringing on big rises of trout.

Grey Midge (Billy Quail)

PLATE 16

Hook: Size 16-18
Tying silk: Black
Body: Close-clipped grizzle cock hackle
Hackle: Grizzle cock

A useful little pattern, especially on the river when small grey midges are being taken by the trout.

Grey Wulff

PLATE 16

Hook: Size 8-12, Partridge L3A
Tying silk: Black
Wing: Brown bucktail tied Wulff-style and divided with the silk
Tail: A small bunch of brown bucktail
Body: Blue rabbit underfur
Hackle: Blue dun cock and ginger cock wound together

The Grey Wulff is especially popular at mayfly time. It was probably first used in Ireland on Lough Derg, where anglers found it equally useful for trout feeding on the green drake and the spent gnat or spinner. The Grey Wulff is only one of a series created by Lee Wulff in the 1930s. I have often seen an Irish version of the Grey Wulff tied using grey squirrel tail for both wing and tail. It appears to be just as effective as the original.

Half Spent Gnat

PLATE 16

Hook: Sizes 8-10, Kamasan B830
Tying silk: Brown
Rib: Oval gold tinsel
Tail: Four fibres of cock pheasant centre tail dyed black
Body: Natural raffia
Body hackle: Short-fibred grizzle cock
Hackle: A long-fibred blue dun cock hackle and a well marked badger cock hackle wound together, with all the fibres then brought to the top of the hook shank in the form of a fan. This is achieved by making a figure-of-eight with the tying silk under the hackle and hook shank

PLATE 16: DRY FLIES

Top Row Ginger Quill, Green Peter, Gold-Ribbed Hare's Ear
1st Row Greenwell's Glory, Greenwell's Parachute, Grey Duster
2nd Row Grey Flag, Grey Wulff, Grey Midge (Quail), Green Midge (Quail)
Bottom Row Half Spent Gnat, Hare's Ear Sedge (Kennedy)

A dressing for either river or lough when the mayfly spinners are returning to the water to lay their eggs.

Hare's Ear Sedge (Micheal Kennedy)

PLATE 16

Hook: Size 10-12, Partridge L3A
Tying silk: Black
Rib: Fine oval gold tinsel
Body: Dark hare's ear
Body hackle: Coch-y-bondhu cock
Wing: Hen pheasant secondary
Front hackle: Ginger cock

When Dr Michael Kennedy described this dressing as 'one of the most useful patterns for Irish waters', I doubt if he realised just how accurate his description was to prove. Maybe this is why he did not give it a name.

I have found it to be one really great fly for both lough and river and it can be fished wet or dry. It is suggestive of several types of sedge and as such will be taken by trout from March to October. Not only will it take trout feeding on sedges, but on the lough it is effective in a lake olive hatch or when buzzers are about, and it will even take trout when no flies at all are on the water. A red-brown body hackle works as well as the coch-y-bondhu.

Hawthorn Fly

PLATE 17

Hook: Size 10-12, Partridge L3A
Tying silk: Black
Rib: Fine silver wire
Body: Black crow herl or black floss
Legs: Two cock pheasant centre tail fibres dyed black, knotted and with the tips cut off
Wings: Two pale blue dun cock hackle tips
Hackle: Black cock

The hawthorn fly (*Bibio marci*) is a terrestrial insect found near hawthorn bushes in the month of May. It is easily spotted as it flies about slowly with long black legs hanging beneath it.

It is a weak flier and can easily get blown on to either river or lake and the trout absolutely love it. This dressing may be fished either wet or dry.

Houghton Ruby

PLATE 17

Hook: Size 14-16, Partridge L3A
Tying silk: Crimson
Tail: White cock hackle fibres
Body: Hackle stalk dyed crimson
Wings: Two light blue dun hackle tips
Hackle: Red game cock.

A pattern to represent the female spinners of the iron blue dun, which are commonest in May but may be encountered on the river at any time in the season.

Humpy

PLATE 17

Hook: Size 10-14, Partridge L3A
Tying silk: Orange
Wing: Elk hair divided Wulff style
Tail/shell back: Brown deerhair
Body: Orange floss with half the tail fibres tied over it
Hackle: Red game cock

An American pattern with exceedingly good floating qualities and very visible. Fish it on the river, on fast water when sedges are about.

Other colours for the body floss and tying silk are: black, brown, red, green and yellow.

Iron Blue Dun

PLATE 17

Hook: Size 16-18, Partridge L3A
Tying silk: Red
Tag: Three turns of the tying silk
Rib: Fine silver wire
Tail: Fibres of dark blue dun hackle
Body: Dark heron herl
Hackle: Dark blue dun cock

Iron blue duns (*Baetis pumilus*) are widespread throughout the country on rivers and streams with medium to fast flowing water. They can hatch anytime from April to November, but are commonest in April and May.

Iron Blue Dun
(Thomas Clegg)

PLATE 17

Hook: Size 16-18, Partridge L3A
Tying silk: Red
Wing: Two lengths of neon magenta and four lengths of horizon blue DRF floss, all tied in together spinner style
Rib: Gold wire
Tail: Dark blue dun cock hackle fibres
Tag: Neon magenta floss
Body: Mole's fur
Hackle: Dark blue dun cock

A good pattern, especially in the month of May if there happens to be a bit of colour in the water.

Jenny Spinner

PLATE 17

Hook: Size 14-16, Partridge L3A
Tying silk: Crimson
Tag: Three turns of tying silk
Tail: Two pale or white microfibetts

Body: Stripped white hackle stalk
Wing: White poly yarn
Thorax: Brown Antron wound over base of wing with a figure-of-eight

An imitation for the male spinner of the iron blue, which sometimes finds its way back on to the surface of the river in the early afternoon.

Kite's Imperial

PLATE 17

Hook: Size 14-16, Partridge L3A
Tying silk: Purple
Rib: Fine gold wire
Tail: Brown hackle fibres early in the season; honey dun hackle fibres from June onwards
Body: Natural heron herl or substitute
Hackle: Honey dun cock

Here is an exceptionally effective pattern and one that I would not be without on the river. It will take trout feeding on large dark olives (*Baetis rhodani*), medium olives (*Baetis tenax*) small dark olives (*Baetis atrebatinus*), olive uprights (*Rithrogena semicolorata*) and even pale wateries (*Centroptilum luteolum*) and yellow evening duns (*Ephemerella notata*). It is one great little fly and if olives are on the water and you are in doubt, give it a try. The response will almost certainly surprise you.

Klinkhamer Special

PLATE 17

Hook: Size 8-14, Partridge K12ST, or GRS12ST, or Tiemco 200R
Tying silk: Fine, 8/0, any pale colour, or Danville's Spider Web
Body: Fine synthetic dubbing of the desired shade, or feather fibre ribbed with fine silver wire

Thorax: Bronze peacock herl
Wing/post: White/grey poly yarn or calf hair
Hackle: A good quality cock hackle - ginger, cree, grizzle, blue dun, or a shade you think appropriate for a given situation

What are we to say of this wonder fly from the vice of the Dutch tyer, Hans van Klinken? I think one fisherman said it all when he commented, 'It makes all other dry flies redundant'. It is fished with the body entirely submerged and the hackle (which is tied around the base of the vertical wing) keeps it afloat. It is not just a single pattern but rather a completely new design, in which a range of dressings can be tied, much in the way of the Wulff series. It can be fished when sedges, buzzers, olives or mayflies are emerging. Before tying, the hook should be bent down slightly about 1/4 inch behind the eye to enable the hackle to lie flat on the surface and the body to hang underwater beneath it.

Lake Olive Dun (Michael Kennedy)

PLATE 17

Hook: Size 12-14, Partridge L3A
Tying silk: Primrose
Rib: Gold wire
Tail: Fibres of ginger cock dyed pale olive
Body: Lightly dubbed olive seal's fur
Hackle: Ginger cock dyed pale olive

This is one of Michael Kennedy's excellent dressings. He advises using the larger size 12 in April and May and a smaller size in September with the body and hackle having a more pronounced golden-olive hue.

Lake Olive Spinner

Trout can sometimes be observed feeding on lake olive spinners in quiet corners and bays in May and September. There are a number of patterns that anglers can try, including the Pheasant Tail, which is probably the best choice. Others are: Lunn's Particular or Little Claret Spinner.

Large Dark Olive

PLATE 17

Hook: Size 12-14, Partridge L3A
Tying silk: Brown olive
Rib: Fine oval gold tinsel
Tail: Hare's body guard hairs
Body: Hare's ear
Hackle: Sooty olive cock

The large dark olive (*Baetis rhodani*) is one of the first of the olives to appear on the river in springtime and hatches may occur at any time throughout the season. It is also important on some rivers in September. The flies are paler and smaller in high summer. The above dressing is just one of several that will take trout feeding on large dark olives. Others are: Brown Olive (page 70), Greenwell's Glory (page 75), Beacon Beige (page 67), and Kite's Imperial (page 79).

The correct shade of hackle is obtained by dying a red game cock cape dark olive.

Large Olive (Peter Brown)

PLATE 17

Hook: Size 14-16, Partridge L3A
Tying silk: Primrose
Rib: Fine flat gold Lurex
Tail: Fibres of stiff grizzle cock
Body: Orange seal's fur or silk
Hackle: Grizzle or furnace cock

A good general pattern favoured by Peter Brown, the former Angling Officer of the Inland Fisheries Trust, when the bigger olives are on the water.

PLATE 17: DRY FLIES

Top Row Hawthorn Fly, Houghton Ruby, Humpy
1st Row Iron Blue Dun (Clegg), Iron Blue Dun, Jenny Spinner
2nd Row Kite's Imperial, Klinkhammer Special, Lake Olive Dun (Kennedy)
Bottom Row Large Dark Olive, Large Olive (Brown), Last Hope (Goddard)

Last Hope (John Goddard)

PLATE 17

Hook: Size 16-18, Partridge L3A
Tying silk: Pale yellow
Tail: Six fibres of honey dun hackle
Body: Buff-coloured goose or condor herl substitute
Hackle: Cream cock, short in fibre

A pattern recommended by John Goddard for use when pale wateries or caenis are on the water.

Light Midge (Andrew Ryan)

PLATE 18

Hook: Size 14-16, Kamasan B170
Tying silk: Black
Tail: Pale blue dun cock
Body: Fine grey and white dubbing, mixed in blender
Hackle: Pale blue dun cock

A useful river pattern when tiny midges are about in daytime. I have observed that when trout are taking the paler midges they will have only the lighter imitation, and *vice versa* with darker midges and their imitation.

Little Claret Spinner

PLATE 18

Hook: Size 14-16, Partridge L3A
Tying silk: Crimson
Rib: Gold wire
Tail: White hackle fibres
Body: Lightly dubbed seal's fur or other fine claret dubbing

This is a useful pattern for evening fishing in May and June on rivers when trout are taking the spinners of medium olives, iron blues, large dark olives, and the green olive (*Ecdyonurus insignis*). It can also be used on lakes in May and September for trout feeding on lake olive spinners (*Cloeon simile*), in sheltered bays in the evening.

Lunn's Particular

PLATE 18

Hook: Size 14-16, Partridge L3A
Tying silk: Crimson
Tail: Fibres of red-brown cock hackle
Body: Hackle stalk stripped (Rhode Island Red or red-brown cock hackle)
Wings: Two medium blue dun cock hackle tips, tied spent
Hackle: Rhode Island Red cock or light red-brown cock

This is a good general pattern for those occasions when red-bodied spinners are on the water.

McGinley's Green Peter

PLATE 18

Hook: Size 8-10, Kamasan B830 or B170
Tying silk: Brown-olive
Tag: DFM green wool
Rib: Fine copper wire
Body: Dark olive seal's fur
Body hackle: Ginger cock
Wing: Mallard duck breast feathers tied on top, saturated with Floo Gloo or clear varnish and moulded into a sedge wing shape with finger and thumb
Hackle: Two ginger cock hackles tied full

This is a dressing by Peter McGinley of Kells for Lough Sheelin. It is tied to represent the big sedges, *Phryganea varia* and *P. obsoleta* (the green peters), which appear in July and August. It is an excellent fly, taking numerous big trout, including one of $8^{1}/_{2}$lbs for its originator.

March Brown

PLATE 18

Hook: Size 12-14 Partridge L3A
Tying silk: Brown-olive
Rib: Olive tying silk
Tail: Fibres of red-brown cock hackle
Body: Hare's ear
Hackle: Brown-olive cock with a couple of turns of grizzle cock wound through it

The march brown (*Rithrogena haarupi*) emerges in March and April on fast, stony, moorland rivers. The hatch can be very prolific but is usually short-lived. This fly occurs only on a few rivers in Ireland.

Medium Olive

PLATE 18

Hook: Size 14-16, Partridge L3A
Tying silk: Primrose
Tail: Ginger cock
Body: Stripped peacock eye quill
Hackle: Medium olive

The medium olive (*Baetis tenax*) is widespread on both fast and slow flowing rivers from mid-April to the end of July. Other useful dressings are: Kite's Imperial (page 79), Greenwell's Glory (page 75), the Wylie (page 96), Ginger Quill (page 74) and the Cul de Canard (page 71).

Mini Wulff

PLATE 18

Hook: Size 12-14, Partridge L3A
Tying silk: Black
Wing: Grey squirrel tail
Tail: Grey squirrel tail
Body: Blue rabbit underfur
Hackle: Grizzle cock dyed picric (lemon yellow)

Fish two of these on a fine leader in the ripple when trout are taking the emerging mayfly on the lough. They can be cast in the vicinity of rising trout but they will also be taken 'on the blind' by trout cruising under the surface in search of hatching duns. Especially good for Lough Conn.

Mosely Mayfly

PLATE 18

Hook: Size 8 or 10, Kamasan B170 or B830
Tying silk: Brown
Rib: Fine oval gold tinsel
Tail: 3-4 fibres of cock pheasant centre tail
Body: Hare's ear and yellow seal's fur mixed in equal parts
Hackle: At shoulder only and tied half circle - in a fan-shape on top of the hook - a medium olive cock hackle and a blue dun cock hackle, with a lemon-yellow cock hackle wound through

This is an excellent pattern for either river or lough when the mayfly (*Ephemera danica*) is hatching and the weather is humid, at which time the naturals may remain on the water for a while and trout will feed on the freshly hatched duns. It appears that this dressing was first tied for Lough Sheelin trout by the late D.E. Mosely of the former Garnett and Keegan's tackle shop in Dublin. The original dressing had a pink hackle, which is very hard to dye. The above dressing is equally effective and Paul Canning of England once won the Brown Bowl with it with 14 trout in an international match on Lough Conn at mayfly time.

Murrough

PLATE 18

Hook: Size 8, Kamasan B830
Tying silk: Brown

PLATE 18: DRY FLIES

Top Row Little Claret Spinner, McGinley's Green Peter, Lunn's Particular
1st Row March Brown, Light Midge (Ryan), Medium Olive
2nd Row Mosely Mayfly, Murrough
Bottom Row Orange Sparkle Dun, Olive Upright, Orange Quill, Mini Wulff

Rib: Fine oval gold
Body: Brown seal's fur
Body hackle: Red-brown cock
Wing: Slips of brown turkey tail tied flat on top of the hook shank and shaped with Floo Gloo
Antennae: Stripped stalks of red-brown hackle
Hackle: Two red-brown cock hackles tied fully round

The murrough (*Phryganea grandis* and *P. striata*) is one of the biggest of our sedges and emerges at dusk and late into the night, from May to July. It occurs on both loughs and on the big quiet pools of limestone rivers. Trout, especially big trout, respond well to it and can provide exciting fishing into the early hours of the morning. Some anglers fish two on a leader, about 4 feet apart.

Olive Upright

PLATE 18

Hook: Size 14-16, Partridge L3A
Tying silk: Primrose
Tail: Medium olive cock hackle fibres
Body: Stripped peacock eye quill dyed olive
Hackle: Medium olive cock

The olive upright (*Rithrogena semicolorata*) is fairly common on east coast rivers and hatches on stony fast-flowing stretches in May and June. Hatches occur either in the afternoon or in the evening. When the spinners are on the water a Pheasant Tail dressed with a honey dun hackle makes an excellent imitation.

Orange Quill

PLATE 18

Hook: Size 12-16, Partridge L3A
Tying silk: Orange

Tail: Natural red cock fibres
Body: Stripped peacock eye quill or a hackle stalk dyed orange
Hackle: Red (natural) Rhode Island cock

This pattern bears little resemblance to the blue-winged olive (*Ephemerella ignita*), yet late in the evening when BWOs are about it is one of the best.

I prefer it tied in the smaller sizes, and have no idea whether is is taken for a dun or a spinner. Billy Quail of Portadown ties the body with orange tying silk and overlaps it with clear PVC. Either way will do.

Orange Sparkle Dun

PLATE 18

Hook: Size 16, Partridge C520
Tying silk: Orange
Wing: Deerhair (sometimes dyed grey)
Tail: Small bunch of white Sparkle Yarn
Body: Orange Lureflash Antron body wool

A dressing by my friend Mike Weaver for the evening BWO hatch. He relates, in his book *The Pursuit of Wild Trout*, how it 'performed magnificently on two June evenings in the prolific BWO hatches of the Suir in Ireland'.

Pale Watery Sparkle Dun

PLATE 19

Hook: Size 16-18, Partridge CS20
Tying silk: Primrose
Wing: Olive dyed deerhair
Tail: White poly yarn
Body: Yellow-olive, fine-textured fur

The pale watery dun (*Centroptilum luteolum*), which is one of the spur-winged Ephemeroptera (also known as the little sky blue), and the pale evening dun (*Procloëon rufulum*) closely resemble each other and for angling purposes the above dressing by

Mike Weaver works equally well for either dun. They are widespread in Ireland and can be observed, especially on rivers, between May and September. They hatch both during the day and at dusk and trout feed freely on them especially on limestone rivers.

The following pattern represents the spinners of both these flies.

Pale Watery Spinner

PLATE 19

Hook: Size 14-16, Partridge L3A
Tying silk: Primrose
Tail: Fibres of white cock hackle
Rib: Fine gold wire
Body: Fine pale yellow dubbing
Wing: White poly yarn tied spent

Pensioner (Andrew Ryan)

PLATE 19

Hook: Size 14-18, Kamasan B170
Tying silk: Grey
Body: Grey poly yarn
Wing: A bunch of grizzle hackle fibres clipped short above the hook bend
Hackle: Grizzle cock

This is a fly for daytime fishing on the river in July and August. Trout take it either for a tiny sedge or a small stonefly and it imitates the profile of the stonefly very well. Fish it on a fine leader. An Andrew Ryan pattern for the River Suir.

Peute

PLATE 19

Hook: Size 12, Kamasan B160
Tying silk: Yellow
Body: Fine white dubbing
Hackle: A dun-coloured mallard feather from underneath the wing, fibres should be

as long as the body of the fly

I am indebted to Andrew Ryan for this dressing and to Robert Dessagne for the fishing instructions for it. The Peute (meaning ugly) is very effective on the Suir and it can be used elsewhere too. This shapeless dressing is at its best in a hatch of olives. It can be fished wet or dry. It is the invention of a Frenchman, Henry Bresson.

Pheasant Tail

PLATE 19

Hook: Size 12-16, Partridge L3A
Tying silk: Brown
Rib: Gold wire
Tail: Fibres of honey dun cock hackle
Body: Cock pheasant centre tail fibres
Hackle: Honey dun cock

This is a really good general-purpose pattern for the river. Trout will take it for a variety of spinners - BWO, iron blue, medium olive and even the lake olive spinner. It can also be dressed with a white or grey poly yarn wing to imitate spent or drowned spinners in the surface film. Try it dressed with a dark blue dun hackle when blue-winged olives are about.

Purcell's Mayfly

PLATE 19

Hook: Size 8-10, Kamasan B830 or B170
Tying silk: Black
Rib: Fine oval gold tinsel
Tail: Four fibres of cock pheasant centre tail
Body: Green olive and golden olive seal's fur mixed, and this in turn is mixed with a pinch of yellow and grey seal's fur
Hackle: A green-olive, a white and a ginger cock hackle wound together at the head

This exceptionally effective pattern was devised for Lough Ennell by Eddie Purcell of

PLATE 19: DRY FLIES

Top Row Pale Watery Sparkle Dun, Pale Watery Spinner, Pensioner
1st Row Peute, Purcell's Mayfly, Pheasant Tail
2nd Row Purple Dun, Red Spinner (Brown), Reed Smut, Red Spinner
Bottom Row Red Quill, Royal Wulff, Rooster

Mullingar. It is probably at its best when trout are taking mayflies off the top and it also works for trout taking the spent gnat. It should be fished dry, on its own, for best results. And just to confirm its attractiveness, it can be fished wet on the top dropper.

Purple Dun

PLATE 19

Hook: Size 12-14, Partridge L3A
Tying silk: Red
Rib: Purple tying silk
Tail: Fibres of dark blue dun hackle
Body: Dark heron herl
Hackle: Dark blue dun cock

The purple dun (*Paraleptophlebia cincta*) occurs sporadically on fast-flowing limestone rivers. J.R. Harris says it is very plentiful on the River Greese in Co. Carlow. It hatches during the day, from May to August, and at times is taken in preference to any other fly on the water.

Red Spinner

PLATE 19

Hook: Size 16-18, Kamasan B405
Tying silk: Crimson
Tail: Fibres of blue dun cock hackle
Body: As tying silk
Hackle: Blue dun cock, rather long and sparsely tied

Some of the female olive spinners climb down a reed, the angler's wader or the like, and lay their eggs underwater and then float to the surface and are carried downstream in the surface film. This was a favourite pattern of the late great Liam O'Farrell, from Cahir on the Suir, for trout feeding on the trapped spinners. Liam's motto was 'Show it to them, and take it away'.

Red Spinner (Peter Brown)

PLATE 19

Hook: Size 16-18, Partridge L3A
Tying silk: Red
Tail: Fibres of honey cock
Body: Red silk
Hackle: Honey cock divided by figure-of-eights with the tying silk so that it lies in the spent position

This is a useful general spinner pattern and Peter Brown finds it works also when sherry spinners are on the water.

Red Quill

PLATE 19

Hook: Size 14-16, Partridge L3A
Tying silk: Red
Tail: Fibres of red game cock
Body: Stripped peacock quill or hackle stalk dyed red
Hackle: Red game

A good general spinner pattern for the river in July and August. It imitates a variety of red-bodied spinners returning to the water to lay their eggs.

Reed Smut (Mike Weaver)

PLATE 19

Hook: Size 20 or 22, Partridge L3A
Tying silk: Black
Body: Fine textured black fur, or substitute
Wing: White poly yarn

When reed smuts (*Simulium spp*) black gnats and black midges are on the water and trout are taking them, it is not the time to be wondering which species is present. What is wanted is a small black fly. If a very small one is called for then try this proven dressing, by Mike Weaver.

Alternatively, you can the rather older Simulium dressing listed on page 90.

Rooster

PLATE 19

Hook: Size 12-16, Kamasan B160
Tying silk: Black
Tail: A bunch of ginger cock hackle fibres
Body: Black floss
Wings: White hackle tips tied spent
Hackle: Ginger cock behind wings and a small cock pheasant body feather tied in at the front

A fly for the fast broken water on the Suir in June. This dressing by Andrew Ryan has also proved its worth on the Boyne.

Royal Wulff

PLATE 19

Hook: Size 8-14, Kamasan B170
Tying silk: Black
Wing: A bunch of calf hair tied in vertically and then divided in a V
Tail: White calf hair or brown bucktail
Body: Bronze peacock herl fore and aft with red floss silk in the middle
Hackle: Ginger cock

At first sight, this gaudy American pattern - another from the series of heavy bodied, buoyant patterns devised by Lee Wulff - would not appear to have much relevance to the anglers of the Emerald Isle. But trout are strange and perverse creatures and the Royal Wulff is a proven taker of trout at mayfly time, especially on Lough Conn and Lough Sheelin.

It can be fished dry in the smaller sizes (e.g. size 12) when the duns are hatching or even on the top dropper on a cast of wet flies. In the bigger sizes (10 and 8) it will take trout feeding on spent gnat at dusk.

Sherry Spinner (Michael Kennedy)

PLATE 20

Hook: Size 14-18, Partridge L3A
Tying silk: Orange
Rib: Gold wire
Tail: Fibres of red-brown cock
Body: Claret and orange seal's fur or substitute mixed in equal parts
Hackle: Blue dun hackle tied spent by dividing it with figure-of-eight turns of the silk. An alternative is grey poly yarn tied spent, with the body material taken over the wing butts

Sherry Spinner

PLATE 20

Hook: Size 14-16, Kamasan B160
Tying silk: Orange
Tail: Fibres of red-brown hackle
Body: Orange-dyed hackle stalk or dark orange floss ribbed with gold wire
Hackle: Natural red game cock

When the female spinners of the blue-winged olive (*Ephemerella ignita*) return to the river - which they do in the evening in high summer and by day in September - it can be important to have a good pattern to match the hatch. This is just such a one.

Silverhorn Sedge

PLATE 20

Hook: Size 10-14
Tying silk: Grey
Rib: Silver wire
Body: Pale olive seal's fur
Wing: Pale grey speckled hen
Antennae: Two fibres of teal flank
Hackle: Grizzled cock

A pattern for the lough when trout are taking silverhorns in July.

Silver Sedge

PLATE 20

Hook: Size 12-14, Partridge L3A
Tying silk: Primrose
Rib: Gold wire
Body: Green-olive seal's fur
Wing: Pale starling wing quill
Hackle: Medium olive

A fly for the river when small pale sedges are about.

Simulium

PLATE 20

Hook: Size 18-22, Partridge L3A
Tying silk: Black
Tag: Flat silver
Body: A strand of bronze peacock herl
Hackle: Black cock

Simulium flies (reed smuts) belong to the order Diptera and the black larvae can sometimes be seen clinging to reeds protruding from the water. The pupa comes up in a bubble of air. The season for Simulium flies is usually from mid-May to the end of June. Trout love them and take the egg laying adults mostly in sheltered eddies and on slow pools. This excellent dressing is by the late Bill Percy of Lurgan and is sometimes called Percy's Black Midge. It has served me, and hundreds of other Northern anglers, well.

Skating Buzzer

PLATE 20

Hook: Size 12 or 14, Partridge L3A
Tying silk: Black
Rib: Silver wire

Tail: Fibres of grizzle cock hackle
Body: Grey seal's fur
Hackle: Grizzle cock, heavily palmered with a couple of turns of hot orange cock tied in at the front

In warm or even hot conditions in May and June buzzers can be observed skating along the lough surface, especially in quiet bays or in the shelter of an island. Trout will sometimes be seen taking these flies as they pause. Michael Kelly, of Balbriggan, has tested this pattern successfully on both Lough Sheelin and Lough Leane.

Small Dark Olive

PLATE 20

Hook: Size 16-18, Partridge L3A
Tying silk: Primrose
Rib: Olive tying silk
Tail: Fibres of grizzle cock
Body: Hare's ear
Hackle: Blue dun cock

The small dark olive (*Baetis scambus*) is widely distributed on both limestone and acid fast-flowing rivers, such as the River Lee. Hatches occur between May and August. This is a very small fly - as small or even smaller than the iron-blue dun - but nonetheless it can bring on a good rise of trout.

Small Olive (Peter Brown)

PLATE 20

Hook: Size 16-18, Partridge L3A
Tying silk: Primrose
Tail: Badger cock hackle fibres
Body: Yellow silk
Hackle: Good-quality Rhode Island Red cock

This is Peter Brown's general river dressing for imitating small olives.

PLATE 20: DRY FLIES

Top Row Sherry Spinner (Kennedy), Silverhorn Sedge, Sherry Spinner
1st Row Silver Sedge, Simulium, Skating Buzzer
2nd Row Small Dark Olive, Spent Gnat (female) Small Olive (Brown)
Bottom Row Spent Gnat (male), Spent Me

Spent Gnat (female)

PLATE 20

Hook: Size 8-10, Kamasan B830
Tying silk: Brown
Rib: Fine oval gold tinsel
Tail: Four fibres of cock pheasant centre tail dyed black
Body: Natural raffia
Body hackle: Short-fibred grizzle or badger cock
Wing: Dark blue dun hackle tips tied spent with long-fibred blue dun cock wound behind the wings and in front and then divided in the spent position with figure-of-eight turns of the silk

When a lot of dead and dying mayfly spinners (*E. danica*) are on the water, trout like a fly that lies properly in the surface film. I have found this dressing as good as any other and it will take trout feeding on spent gnats both during the day and at dusk. It was this dressing that won the Lough Conn Mayfly Competition for John Murphy in the early 1990s. Fish either a single fly, or two at a time (four feet apart on the leader).

Spent Gnat (male)

PLATE 20

Hook: Size 10, Kamasan B830
Tying silk: Black
Rib: Gold wire
Tail: Four fibres of cock pheasant centre tail dyed black
Body: White herl (turkey or goose)
Body hackle: Short-fibred white cock
Wing: Black cock hackle tied spent

It happens occasionally at mayfly time that the male spinners of *E. danica* fall on to the water in sufficient numbers for trout to feed on them. On a lough, they usually fall close in to the shore and, while this *can* happen in the evening, it is more likely to occur in the early morning.

Spent Mc

PLATE 20

Hook: Size 8-10, Partridge GSSH
Tying silk: Black
Wings: Grey squirrel hair tied in the semi-spent position
Rib: Fine gold wire closely ribbed
Tail: Grey squirrel
Body: Hare's body fur
Undercarriage: Cock pheasant tail fibres
Hackle: A grizzle and a black cock hackle wound together

There are not many anglers who have caught more big trout on Lough Sheelin than Stuart McTeare, who incidentally holds the record (11lb 7oz) for the biggest fly-caught Sheelin trout. He operates a good guest-house and angling centre on the lough at Finea. This is his favourite pattern when spent gnat (mayfly spinners) are on the water. It started life as a Grey Wulff but the final mutation is definitely more gnatty. The undercarriage is like a wing case but is tied under the hook and divides the hackle. This is a pattern of proven worth.

Suir Beauty (Andrew Ryan)

PLATE 21

Hook: Size 10-14, Kamasan B160
Tying silk: Black
Tail: Fibre of honey dun cock hackle
Body: Rear half, grey Antron; front half, lemon-yellow Antron
Hackle: Honey dun cock

A dressing of Andrew Ryan's for April-May on the Suir and Nire.

Sunset Red Spinner
(Thomas Clegg)

PLATE 21

Hook: Size 16-12, Partridge L3A
Tying silk: Primrose
Wing: Two lengths each of neon magenta, Arc Chrome, and horizon blue DRF floss, all tied in together, spinner style.
Tail: Fibres of red-brown cock hackle
Body: Tightly turned fine orange DRF floss
Hackle: Red-brown cock

Recommended for midsummer nights on the river, especially at sunset when trout are rising to emerging BWOs. Billy Quail says it can give phenomenal results and trout will take it when the light has gone and the angler can no longer see the fly.

Sunshine Spent Gnat

PLATE 21

Hook: Size 10, Partridge EIA
Tying silk: Brown
Tail: Three fibres of dyed black cock pheasant centre tail
Rib: Brown tying silk
Body: Hook shank painted white with a slip of white duck or swan tied underneath behind the wing to lie beneath the hook and extend beyond the bend
Wing: A white hackle wound behind a dark blue dun hackle, both divided by figure-of-eight turns of the silk to hold them in the spent position

This is a dressing by the late Dr Patterson from Northern Ireland. He fished it with great success at mayfly time on Lough Carra, and especially during the day, as its name suggests. I also saw him take a good bag of trout with it one day on Lough Arrow. He tied the original on light gold-plated hooks.

Tricolore No.1

PLATE 21

Hook: Size 12-14, Kamasan B160
Tying silk: Black
Hackles: Palmered insequence from the back: grey, red game and badger (in front)

The Tricolore is one of the best-known French river flies and was named by André Ragot, who recognised its advantages of being very visible *and* a good floater. It is especially good on streamy water and is a favourite of Andrew Ryan's for the Suir.

For the Tricolore No.2 substitute a black hackle for the badger; for the Tricolore No.3, a yellow hackle.

Tup's Indispensable

PLATE 21

Hook: Size 14-16, Partridge L3A
Tying silk: Primrose
Tail: Fibres of honey dun cock hackle
Body: Rear half, primrose tying silk; front half, tup's wool mixture or lemon-yellow and pink dubbing fur mixed
Hackle: Honey dun cock

A pattern that is well worth a try when pale wateries or their spinners are on the river on summer evenings.

Two Feather Mayfly

PLATE 21

Hook: Size 12, Partridge L3A
Tying silk: Black
Tail, body and wing: Take a dyed lemon-yellow mallard drake flank feather and snip out the centre about 1 cm up from the point. Now draw all the fibres except the last two on either side towards the base of the stalk. This gives the tail and the body. Tie in on top of the hook shank and bring a few

turns of silk in front to hold the wing vertical. Snip out the stalk
Hackle: Badger cock wound in front and behind the wing

Here is a fly that is very nearly as light as a feather and floats well. It has worked like a dream for me on Lough Mask when trout were taking mayflies in the big wave in front of a drifting boat, as well as in the calmer bays and inlets. It also works well on many rivers and is a particular favourite with anglers on the Boyne.

Werewolf (Michael Kelly)

PLATE 21

Hook: Size 8 or 10, Kamasan B170
Tying silk: Black
Rib: Gold wire
Tag: Green DFM floss
Body: Claret seal's fur
Body hackle: Red-brown cock
Wing: Brown bucktail trimmed to shape
Hackle: Two red brown cock hackles inter-wound with lots of turns
Antennae: Two fibres of cock pheasant tail

A dressing by Michael Kelly to be fished dry on the loughs from late May onwards when dark brown sedges or murroughs are on the water.

Welshman's Button

PLATE 21

Hook: Size 10-12, Kamasan B170
Tying silk: Black
Rib: Gold wire
Body: Grey seal's fur with a little olive seal's fur mixed through
Wings: Three mallard drake brown neck feathers tied in and varnished Devaux style (see Devaux Sedge, page 72)
Hackle: Red-brown cock

The Welshman's button (*Sericostoma personatum*) is fairly widespread on rivers and even loughs (for example, Lough Ennell) during the day from late May to August. It can be big, up to 15mm long, and is recognisable by its dark or chestnut-brown wings.

White Moth

PLATE 22

Hook: Size 10-12
Tying silk: Primrose
Rib: Silver wire
Body: White chenille
Hackle: White cock
Wing: Slips of white duck

Moths flutter and try to take off again when they land on a pool at night, and so a well hackled dressing is called for.

Williams Favourite

PLATE 22
Hook: Size 14-16, Partridge L3A
Tying silk: Black
Rib: Fine silver wire
Tail (optional): Black cock hackle fibres
Body: Black floss silk
Hackle: Black cock

When black gnats are on a lough, trout will often home in on them and look at nothing else. They are generally found along sheltered shores or in the margins, between ripple and calm, in late May, June and July. In this situation, anchor or pull the boat up on the shore and try a Williams Favourite on a fine leader. This tactic certainly works on both Lough Sheelin and Lough Owel.

PLATE 21: DRY FLIES

Top Row Suir Beauty (Ryan), Sunshine Spent Gnat, Sunset Red Spinner (Clegg)
1st Row Tricolore No.1, Tup's Indispensable
2nd Row Two Feather Mayfly, Welshman's Button
Bottom Row Two Feather Mayfly, Werewolf

Willow Fly

PLATE 22

Hook: Size 14, Partridge L3A
Tying silk: Yellow
Body: Mole fur
Wing: Slips of dark starling quill tied sedge-style and soaked with Floo Gloo
Hackle: Dark honey dun cock

Some rivers, such as the Boyne, get big hatches of stoneflies (*Plecoptera*) or needle flies (*Leuctra*) which are slate grey in colour. If trout are feeding on them try this Alfred Ronalds dressing, well greased and fished in the surface film. Alternatively, an Orange Grouse (fished wet) will sometimes take a fish at this time.

Wylie

PLATE 22

Hook: Size 14-16, Partridge L3A
Tying silk: Black
Rib: Gold wire
Tail: Pale blue dun cock
Body: Stripped peacock eye quill
Hackle: A pale blue dun and a red game cock interwound

This is, I believe, a Northern Ireland pattern and it is an excellent fly when medium olives are on the water. It is also a good general pattern for a whole range of olives.

Yellow Evening Dun

PLATE 22

Hook: Size 14-16, Partridge L3A
Tying silk: Primrose
Rib: Fine gold wire
Tail: Honey dun cock hackle fibres
Body: Fine pale yellow dubbing
Hackle: Cree or honey cock

The yellow evening dun (*Ephemerella notata*) is about from about mid-May to mid-June. It is plentiful on the Boyne, Kells Blackwater, Liffey and upper Nore, but may occur elsewhere on the faster stretches of rivers. The hatch begins around sunset and usually lasts for an hour or so.

Yellow Evening Dun Spinner

PLATE 22

Hook: Size 14-16, Partridge L3A
Tying silk: Primrose
Rib: Fine gold wire
Tail: Fibres of honey dun cock
Body: Fine amber/yellow dubbing
Hackle: Honey dun cock

These spinners can often be found on the river about an hour before sunset, from mid-May to mid-June.

Yellow May Dun

PLATE 22

Hook: Size 14-16, Partridge L3A
Tying silk: Primrose
Rib: Fine gold wire
Tail: Honey dun cock
Body: Fine yellow dubbing
Hackle: A yellow and honey dun hackle interwound

The yellow may dun (*Heptagenia sulphurea*) is often mistakenly called the yellow sally or yellow hawk. It is fairly widespread throughout the country and very easy to spot. The hatch is usually sparse and occurs from May onwards. Trout will often ignore them but if the hatch becomes more plentiful it will prompt a rise, especially in the evening. The Kells Blackwater is one river where I have seen this happen.

Yellow May Dun
(Peter Brown)

PLATE 22

Hook: Size 12-16, Partridge L3A
Tying silk: Primrose
Rib: Fine gold wire
Tail: Fibres of honey dun cock hackle
Body: Yellow seal's fur
Hackle: Honey dun cock or pale blue dun

This is a versatile pattern. Peter Brown of Dublin devised it and he finds it particularly effective when trout are feeding on yellow may duns (*H. sulphurea*) and yellow evening duns (*E. notata*).

Yellow May Spinner

PLATE 22

Hook: Size 14, Partridge L3A
Tying silk: Orange
Tail: Fibres of honey cock hackle
Rib: Gold wire
Body: Yellow dubbing
Wing: White poly yarn, tied spent

A standard dressing for the spinner of the yellow may dun.

PLATE 22: DRY FLIES

Top Row Williams Favourite, White Moth, Willow Fly
Middle Row Wylie, Yellow Evening Dun Spinner, Yellow Evening Dun
Bottom Row Yellow May Dun, Yellow May Spinner, Yellow May Dun (Brown)

The Salmon Flies

Ireland has a long tradition of classic or fully dressed salmon flies. Obviously they have caught a great many fish in their time. There are still anglers who like to fish them today in certain situations which is why I have included a selection of the more popular ones here. The dressings of some of these fully-dressed flies have had to be abridged. This is because the most popular sizes for them are 6 and 8 and it is virtually impossible to get all the traditional materials on to hooks of this size. Another reason for abridgement is that some of the exotic materials used in days past are now no longer available or allowed by law.

Hairwinged salmon flies are increasingly popular and many of the dressings listed here are internationally known. I suspect that the badger series of flies have their origins in Ireland.

SHRIMP FLIES FOR SALMON

Shrimp Flies are immensely popular and so I think it only right to deal with them in some detail.

The Salmon Shrimp Fly was invented and named by the late Pat Curry of Coleraine, who tied the original Curry's Red Shrimp. Such was its success that it has begotten a whole series of salmon flies for different rivers and water and light conditions. The variations on the theme of the Shrimp Fly are now so numerous that it is probably the most popular salmon fly used in Ireland at the present time. This, of course, is a tribute to its effectiveness in almost all conditions.

The style of dressing is characterised by a golden pheasant red or yellow breast feather for a tail. The body is usually in two halves, separated by a hackle. The wing is two jungle cock feathers with a hackle wound full circle in front and the head may be red or black.

Single, double and treble hooks are widely used to dress Shrimp Flies. Trebles are popular for rivers, and singles are the norm on the lough. Size 6 is occasionally used for heavy water in spring or autumn, but the lighter size 8 treble will usually work in these conditions too. Size 10 trebles are the most popular and are about right for 90 percent of the time. Size 12 trebles are sometimes used in low water.

Many anglers make the mistake of fishing too big a Shrimp Fly.

In all the standard shrimp dressings, the golden pheasant breast feather used for the tail is wound on like a hackle. This creates a fly which has movement and life. Tie in the selected feather by the base (or stalk), grip the tip with the hackle pliers, wind it around the hook shank, and then tie it in and snip off the waste three or four centre fibres.

The length of the tail is determined by the length of the fibres of the feather chosen and this determines the overall length of the fly. Ideally, I think the tail should be $^1/_4$ - $^3/_8$ inch (5-10mm) longer than the hook shank, from the tip of the eye to the back of the bend, but some prefer them shorter.

Both oval and flat tinsel are used for tags and ribbing. This is often a matter of personal preference. Oval tags help to maintain the splay of the tail whilst flat tags shine through it better. Some tyers use flat tinsel tags with a small turn of seal's fur in front in order to improve the splay of the tail.

The middle hackle may be either a soft cock or a hen. It should be doubled before being tied in. Length is important and the tips of the fibres should reach the back of the bend of the hook or extend $^1/_4$ inch (6-7mm) beyond. The middle hackle should sit sloped back, but well out from the shank.

The body may be dressed half and half but a better style of dressing is to have the rear part three-fifths and the front part two-fifths the length of the body. When judging these proportions it is important to take into account the space required for the front hackle and head.

Flies with flat tinsel bodies or bodies formed of touching turns of oval tinsel should have the body laid down on a tacky clear varnish base for durability and the finished body should also be varnished, with oval tinsel bodies getting two coats of varnish. Always ensure that there are no gaps left in a flat tinsel or oval tinsel body. This is best achieved by laying down a flat base with the tying silk.

The original method of tying in the jungle cock wings is still thought to be the best way. They were tied in after the body was finished. Traditionally, the jungle cock wings were tied in a style called roofing with the tips extending mid-way between the middle hackle and the tail. On single hooks, the tips of the two feathers are sometimes stuck together on the top edge with clear varnish, Floo Gloo or Super Glue. They are tied in each with one stem on either side of the hook. They thus slope backwards and upwards. This style is not so much used on double or treble hooks where the two feathers are tied in, often on either side of the eye, and split apart to form a V, sloping slightly upwards.

On the bigger flies, if large jungle cock wings are not thought desirable, then smaller jungle cock feathers are tied in as 'cheeks' or even as 'eyes' after the front hackle has been tied in.

In the case of smaller flies (say sizes 10 and 12), the jungle cock is often tied in as eyes after the front hackle and on top of the hook but still with a pronounced 'V'. The front hackle should extend two-thirds of the way back over the middle hackle, reaching to about the point of the hook. It is doubled and tied sloping well back to give a streamlined effect which is very important to avoid skating when the fly is finished.

Heads are usually black or red in colour, but this is largely a matter of personal choice. A coat of thin, clear varnish should be applied first and allowed to dry, as this prevents the finished colour from running through the hackle.

LOW WATER SHRIMPS

Most shrimp dressings can also be tied in low water style and here the object is to tie a slimmer fly rather than a shorter one.

In dressing a Low Water Shrimp, the tail and hackles are not wound. Instead, sparse pinches of fibres are tied in on top of and under the hook shank - in beard-hackle style. The tail fibres will be slightly shorter. The body is dressed the same length as for a standard fly but floss silk is used instead of seal's fur. The tag is flat tinsel and the rib fine oval tinsel. The wing is constructed of a single fairly big jungle cock feather split into two or three slips. These slips are bunched together and tied in on top of the hook. The hook is usually a low-water single or double iron. The fly is often fished on the slower pools by casting up and across and stripping slowly back. The Claret Tail Bann Special is regarded as one of the best shrimp flies for taking jaded fish in low water when dressed in low water style, and it once took twelve fish for an angler in an afternoon.

There is a commonly held belief abroad that shrimp flies only work in Ireland and that they are at their best for late summer and back-end fishing. This is not so. Shrimp flies from Ireland have been used with outstanding success in Scotland and the north of England rivers. As regards the time of year, salmon in a river will take a shrimp fly as freely as any other pattern, when the water is right, from the very start of the season.

The River Mourne shrimp flies are beautiful creations and tied in a particular style. Seal's fur is nearly always used, and in rich shades. The tinsel colour is always varied, with gold at the rear and silver in front.

Certain rules must be observed if shrimp flies are to be fished successfully. First, the size must be right. The biggest mistake is to fish too big a fly. Then the fly must be worked to give it life. This is usually done with the rod tip. In slacker flows the fly should be worked in short darts and in faster flows it should be jigged less frequently around the arc, with the current doing most of the work.

Robert Gillespie, the renowned gillie, flytyer and bait-maker on the Moy, considers the top ten shrimp patterns to be:

1. Bann Special
2. Foxford Shrimp (Light)
3. Faughan Shrimp (Dark)
4. Orange & Gold Shrimp
5. Agivey Wye Bug No.1

6. Claret Shrimp
7. Yellow Shrimp
8. Claret Tail Bann Shrimp
9. Silver Shrimp
10. White Shrimp

Agivey Wye Bug No.1

PLATE 25

Hook: Size 6-12 treble, double or single
Tag: Flat or oval silver
Tail: Golden pheasant red breast feather
Rear body: Orange seal's fur
Rib: Oval silver tinsel
Middle hackle: Hot orange
Front body: Black seal's fur
Rib: Oval silver tinsel
Wings: Jungle cock
Front hackle: Red game or light brown
Head: Black

Agivey Wye Bug No.2

PLATE 25

Hook: Size 6-12 treble, double or single
Tag: Flat or oval silver
Tail: Golden pheasant red breast feather
Rear body: Orange seal's fur
Rib: Oval silver tinsel
Middle hackle: Hot orange
Front body: Black seal's fur
Rib: Oval silver tinsel
Wings (or eyes in small sizes): Jungle cock
Front hackle: Black
Head: Black

Agivey Wye Bug No.3

PLATE 25

Hook: Size 6-12 treble, double or single
Tag: Flat or oval silver
Tail: Golden pheasant red breast feather
Body: Half red and half black seal's fur jointed body, red at rear
Rib: Oval silver tinsel
Front hackle 1: Longish hot orange hen tied sloping back veiling body
Wings: Jungle cock tied split as wings or roofed between hackles

PLATE 23: SALMON FLIES

Top Row Badger, Badger & Orange, Black & Orange
1st Row Black & Yellow, Black Dart, Dunkeld
2nd Row Exe Tube, Towy Tube, Garry Dog
Bottom Row Green Highlander, Goshawk

Front hackle 2: Red game or light brown
Head: Black

Agivey Wye Bug No.4

PLATE 25

Hook: Size 6-12 treble, double or single
Tag: Flat or oval silver tinsel
Tail: Golden pheasant red breast feather
Rear body: Red floss
Rib: Oval silver tinsel
Middle hackle: Hot orange
Front body: Black floss
Rib: Oval silver tinsel
Wings: Roofed jungle cock
Front hackle: Red game or light brown
Head: Black

Agivey Wye Bug No.5

PLATE 25

Another popular Moy version for resident or jaded fish, much toned down.

Hook: Size 10 or 12 treble, double or single
Tag: Oval silver tinsel
Tail: Golden pheasant, red breast feather
Rear body: Orange seal's fur
Rib: Fine flat silver or oval silver
Middle hackle: Smaller red golden pheasant breast feather
Front body: Black seal's fur
Rib: Oval silver tinsel
Front hackle: Black
Eyes: Small jungle cock
Head: Black

There are many variations of the Agivey Wye Bug, which is probably the most popular Shrimp Fly pattern in Ireland. The Agivey Wye Bug No.1 is generally regarded as the original pattern and is a great fly in any season and any water or weather conditions for either fresh or jaded fish. It is popular throughout Ireland. The

front hackle can be varied considerably, according to personal preference. It can be light, medium or dark red game, dyed dark or light brown, furnace, or dark Greenwell.

The Agivey Wye Bug No.2, is popular in Northern Ireland and is popular also as a lough fly. Numbers 3 and 5 are popular west of Ireland variations.

No.3 has a non-standard body style and is slightly easier to tie than the others. Some anglers consider it the most effective of the Wye Bug dressings. A good all-round fly, it is probably at its best on a dull day.

No.4 is the one that is usually tied commercially and it is widely used for this reason.

No.5 uses a golden pheasant red breast feather as a middle hackle and on its day it can really move difficult jaded fish. It is only used in the smaller sizes (10s and 12s), and is popular on the Moy.

Ally's Shrimp

PLATE 25

Hook: Size 4-12, single, double or treble
Tying silk: Red
Rib: Oval silver tinsel
Tail: Small bunch of hot orange bucktail
Body: Rear half, red floss; front half, black floss
Underwing: Bunch of natural grey squirrel
Overwing: Golden pheasant tippets
Beard hackle: Natural grey squirrel tail
Hackle: Hot orange, long in fibre
Head: Red

This pattern by Alastair Gowans has become very popular in recent years. It will take fish from late spring to late autumn and can be fished on a sunk, intermediate, sink-tip or floating line, depending on water temperature and light.

Apache Shrimp
(Albert Atkins)

PLATE 25

Hook: Size 6-12 single, double or treble
Tag: Flat or oval silver
Tail: Golden pheasant red breast feather
Rear body: Golden yellow floss
Rib: Oval silver
Middle hackle: Golden yellow soft cock or hen
Front body: Scarlet floss
Rib: Oval silver
Front hackle: Scarlet soft cock or hen
Head: Black

The Apache Shrimp was invented and named by Albert Atkins, the well-known Garvagh fly dresser. It was his secret weapon long before he released it and it is now widely used from the Lower Bann all the way to the Moy and beyond. It is a particular favourite on the Lackagh River.

Badger (Christopher Pringle)

PLATE 26

Hook: Size 3/4 - 2 inch Waddington shank
Rib: Flat silver tinsel
Body: Black floss silk
Wing: Badger hair tied all round
Sides: Two cock hackle tips, orange, red, yellow or blue
Head: Black

An effective pattern tied by Christopher Pringle of Monaghan and fished successfully on the Slaney, Erriff, Owenmore, Drowes and no doubt many other rivers as well. It can be fished effectively on a sunk line, even in summer. The most popular side colours are orange and yellow.

THE BADGER SHRIMPS

Badger & Orange Shrimp

PLATE 26

Hook: Size 6-12 treble, double or single
Tag: Oval or flat silver
Tail: Golden pheasant red breast feather, wound
Rear body: Orange seal's fur
Rib: Oval or flat silver
Middle hackle: Creamy badger
Front body: Black seal's fur
Rib: Oval silver
Front hackle: Creamy badger
Head: Red

A rear body of red seal's fur makes a Badger and Red Shrimp; and golden olive seal's fur is used for the Badger and Golden Olive Shrimp. These are very simple but very effective patterns. Optional hackle-tip veilings may be used at the middle hackle, of the same colour as the seal's fur.

These are ideal patterns for the beginner to flytying and there are very few occasions when these flies will not take fish just as successfully as more complex patterns. They are simple to tie, and effective to fish. Dark-cream-tipped badger hackles must be used in each dressing. They are excellent in dull weather or a dropping spate but are not recommended for very bright days.

Ballina Grey Shrimp

PLATE 27

Hook: Size 6-12, treble, double or single
Tag: Flat or oval copper tinsel
Tail: Golden pheasant red breast feather
Rear body: Orange floss
Rib: Oval copper
Middle hackle: White
Front body: Dark blue floss

PLATE 24: SALMON FLIES

Top Row Moy Green, Munro Killer (Dark), Munro Killer (Light)
1st Row Shrimp Fly, Wilkinson, Silver Badger
2nd Row Stoat's Tail, Silver Stoat
Bottm Row Thunder & Lightning, Willie Gunn

PLATE 25: SALMON FLIES
Top Row Agivey Wye Bug No.1, Agivey Wye Bug No.2
1st Row Agivey Wye Bug No.3
2nd Row Agivey Wye Bug No.4, Agivey Wye Bug No.5
3rd Row Apache Shrimp
Bottom Row Ally's Shrimp, Blue Shrimp

Rib: Oval copper tinsel
Front hackle: Badger or grizzle
Head: Black

This is a local pattern, much used on the tidal waters of the Moy, particularly in September. It works well on dull, squally, rainy days.

Ballynahinch Badger

PLATE 27

Hook: Size 4-10, single or double
Tag: Fine round silver tinsel and yellow floss
Rib: Oval silver tinsel
Tail: Golden pheasant topping
Body: Black floss
Hackle: Kingfisher blue cock
Wing: Badger hair
Head: Black

I like to refer to this fly as the Ballynahinch Badger to avoid any confusion. It was first given to me by Michael Conneely, that knowledgeable and great salmon fisher and manager of the Ballynahinch Castle Hotel Fishery in Connemara. It is the first fly Michael will recommend to a guest and I believe it is one of the most effective flies you can fish for fresh salmon in clear water. A size 8 single is probably the most useful in summer. I like to fish it on a floating line and find it especially useful for inducing a take when retrieving line by hand in the slower water at the tail of a stream. Very much a fresh-fish and early-season fly.

Bann Special Shrimp

PLATE 27

Hook: Size 6-12, treble, double or single
Tag: Flat or oval silver
Tail: Golden pheasant red breast feather
Rear body: Yellow floss or yellow seal's fur
Rib: Oval silver

Middle hackle: Hot orange
Front body: Black floss or black seal's fur
Rib: Oval silver
Wings: Split or roofed jungle cock
Front hackle: Badger cock
Head: Black

This is a pattern from the lower Bann and is regarded by many as one of the most effective shrimp patterns, being excelled only by the Foxford Shrimp when conditions are really difficult. It is successful everywhere, in all seasons and weather and water conditions, for both fresh and resident fish. Seal's fur is preferred to floss silk for the body.

Black Doctor

PLATE 27

Hook: Size 4-10, single or double
Tag: Fine oval silver tinsel and lemon yellow floss
Tail: Golden pheasant topping and Indian crow substitute
Butt: Red wool
Rib: Oval silver tinsel
Body: Black floss
Hackle: Dark claret cock from second turn of the rib
Throat: Speckled guinea-fowl
Wing: Tippet in strands; married red, blue and yellow swan, bustard, peacock wing and light mottled turkey; narrow strips of teal or summer duck; brown mallard over and topping over all
Head: Red varnish

What salmon fisher could afford not to have one of these flies in his fly box? It is an old tried and trusted pattern and may well contain features that makes it especially attractive to salmon.

Fish the Black Doctor on an overcast day and don't be afraid to give it a try on the river towards the end of the season. A good fly for spring fish on the lough on dull days.

Black Goldfinch

PLATE 27

Hook: Size 4-10 single, or size 2-10 double
Tag: Fine round silver tinsel and orange floss
Tail: Golden pheasant topping and Indian crow substitute
Butt: Black ostrich
Rib: Oval silver tinsel
Body: Black floss
Hackle: Claret cock from second turn of the rib (from the rear)
Throat: Blue jay
Wing: Married slips of yellow and red swan or goose with a topping over

I have been made aware of this pattern for as long as I have fished the west of Ireland. It was favoured by older anglers on Corrib and Lough Beltra in its original dressing and is still used on the Slaney for spring fish dressed on 2/0 and 3/0 irons.

Experienced fishermen at Castleconnell hold a hairwing version in high esteem. There, it is dressed with a really bulky wing of yellow bucktail - big enough to give the heavy Castleconnell fish something worthwhile to aim at.

Black & Orange Tube Fly

PLATE 26

Tube: From 3/4 to 3 inches
Rib: Embossed silver tinsel
Body: Black floss silk
Wing: Two bunches of orange bucktail and two bunches of black bucktail

A dressing for either spring or autumn when there is a bit of colour in the water and the light is good.

Black Shrimp

PLATE 26

Hook: Size 6-12 treble, double or single
Tag: Flat or oval silver tinsel
Tail: Long black cock hackle, wound, or a slim bunch of black hair
Rear body: Fluorescent yellow floss or plain yellow floss
Rib: Medium oval silver
Middle hackle: Hot orange
Front body: Black floss
Rib: Fine oval silver
Front hackle: Black
Eyes (optional): Small jungle cock
Head: Black

This is definitely a low-water fly. It is good for resident fish in August and September and is best used in small sizes. The Black Shrimp is thought to have originated on the River Ness in Scotland but is now popular in Ireland.

Black & Silver Shrimp

PLATE 26

Hook: Size 6-12, treble, double or single
Tag: Oval silver
Tail: Golden pheasant red breast feather, wound
Rear body: Flat silver
Rib: Oval silver
Middle hackle: Black
Front body: Flat silver
Rib: Oval silver
Wings: Roofed jungle cock
Front hackle: Black
Throat: Blue jay, or guinea-fowl dyed blue
Head: Black

This fly has its origins in Northern Ireland. It is a great fly for fresh grilse fly and a good evening fly. It will take fish at any time of the season and is particularly good on the

Moy estuary beats in late summer. In the smaller sizes it can be tied with a one-piece body and a black hen hackle at the front.

Black & Yellow Tube Fly

PLATE 26

Tube: From 1/2 to 3 inches
Rib: Embossed silver tinsel
Body: Black floss
Wing: Black bucktail on top and yellow bucktail underneath

A fly for clear water and any light conditions. Dressed on a 11/2 inch brass tube and fished on a floating line, it will take fish in bright sunshine, even in high summer, as I witnessed at Delphi in the 1995 June heatwave.

Beltra Badger

PLATE 27

Hook: Size 4-10 single or double
Tag: Fine round silver tinsel and yellow floss
Tail: Golden pheasant topping
Butt: Black ostrich herl
Rib: Oval silver tinsel
Body: Flat silver tinsel
Hackle: Lemon yellow from the second turn of the tinsel
Throat: Kingfisher blue cock
Wing: Badger hair over a few fibres of red bucktail with a topping over all
Head: Black

The origination of this fly is attributed to Martin Maguire of Newport, County Mayo. As the name suggests, it was designed for salmon fishing on Lough Beltra and anyone contemplating fishing for spring salmon there should not be without one. It gave me three spring fish there one April evening in less than an hour. It is usually dressed on a single hook and fished on the dropper in

size 8 or 6, but occasionally a size 4 is used in March. It is a great favourite at Delphi dressed on a size 10 double.

Blue Charm

PLATE 27

Hook: Size 4-10 single or double
Tag: Fine round silver tinsel and yellow floss
Rib: Oval silver tinsel
Tail: Golden pheasant topping
Body: Black floss
Hackle: Kingfisher blue
Wing: Tippet in strands, strips of bronze mallard partly covered with strips of teal topping over all. (A hairwing version may be tied using grey squirrel tail as a wing)

When I think of the Blue Charm I am reminded of the Icelandic gillie who banned the Blue Charm from his fly box because he considered it too deadly. It is at its best when the water is perfectly clear. It is as effective on the east coast rivers as on the west coast and I like it, especially, on bright days with a bit of blue in the sky and the sun flitting fitfully in and out of the clouds. Try it early in the morning and dont be afraid to use a size 10 or 12 double in low water in summer.

Blue Shrimp

PLATE 25

Hook: Size 6-12 treble, double or single
Tag: Fine oval silver tinsel
Tail: Golden pheasant red breast feather wound
Rear body: Orange floss
Rib: Oval silver
Middle hackle: Medium or dark blue
Front body: Black floss
Rib: Oval silver
Wings: Roofed jungle cock
Front hackle: Badger

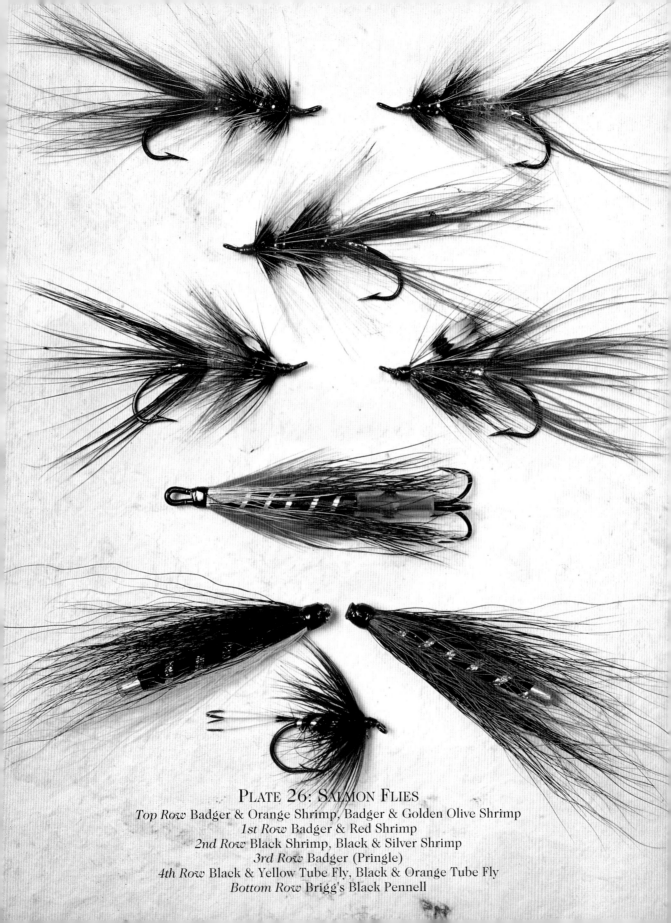

PLATE 26: SALMON FLIES
Top Row Badger & Orange Shrimp, Badger & Golden Olive Shrimp
1st Row Badger & Red Shrimp
2nd Row Black Shrimp, Black & Silver Shrimp
3rd Row Badger (Pringle)
4th Row Black & Yellow Tube Fly, Black & Orange Tube Fly
Bottom Row Brigg's Black Pennell

Head: Black or red

This fly is also known as the Blue Hackle Jock Scott Shrimp or the Blue Hackle Shrimp. It is a great fly in any conditions for very fresh fish and was the fly used by two anglers on the Ridge Pool on the Moy to take so many fish in one session that when the photograph of the catch was published it caused a storm in the angling press. It is often tied in size 10 without the jungle cock and with a rich dark kingfisher blue hackle. Not so good for resident fish.

Botham's Fancy

PLATE 27

Hook: Size 8 and 10, but I prefer to tie it on size 10 and 12 Esmond Drury trebles
Tying silk: Primrose
Tag: Fine oval silver tinsel
Rib: Oval silver tinsel
Body: DFM green floss
Hackle: A bunch of Cambridge blue hackle fibres tied in at the throat
Wing: Black squirrel

I first tied this fly for a visit by Ian Botham, the English cricket player, to Ballynahinch in 1987. It was an instant success and achieved the desired result, so much so that everyone in the hotel wanted one as well. It has had its days too on the Erriff and on the Moy when the grilse are running and is sometimes mistakenly referred to these as The Ridge Pool Special.

Briggs' Pennell

PLATE 26

Hook: Size 8-12 Partridge L2A
Tying silk: Black
Rib: Flat silver tinsel
Tail: Golden pheasant tippets
Body: Black seal's fur well picked out

Hackle: Natural black hen, long in fibre, three or four turns

Dr Francis Briggs, of East Grinstead, Sussex, tied this fly for the River Erriff in Co. Mayo, which he has fished for salmon for nearly thirty years. This is probably his most productive fly. It is at its best in windy conditions with a ripple or wave on the deeper pools and is fished on the dropper on a two-fly leader on a floating or sinking line. It is one pattern every west coast salmon angler should have in his fly box. With it, Dr Briggs has made a significant contribution to salmon flyfishing on spate rivers.

Canadian Green

PLATE 28

Hook: Size 6-10 single or double
Tying silk: Black
Tag: Fine oval silver tinsel
Rib: Fine oval silver tinsel
Tail: Golden pheasant topping
Body: DFM green floss
Wing: Grey squirrel tail dyed green
Hackle: Yellow cock tied as a collar

This is a dressing by Warren Duncan of New Brunswick and it is especially good for fresh fish. Dr Ken Whelan of Burrishoole rates it highly and finds it especially effective on The Neck beat of his fishery. I prefer it tied on small double hooks, with sizes 10 and 12 being particularly good.

Claret & Jay

PLATE 28

Hook: Sprite single size 6-10, or Partridge Low Water Wilson size 12-14
Tag: Fine round silver tinsel and orange floss
Tail: Golden pheasant tippets and topping
Rib: Oval silver tinsel

Hackle: Dark claret cock
Throat: Blue jay
Wing: Tippet in strands under bronze mallard

This old pattern - probably from Donegal - is as useful today as when it was first invented. It is attractive but not gaudy and I like to fish it in smaller sizes dressed on double hooks. It works well in a ripple on the deep, slow pools.

Claret Shrimp

PLATE 28

Hook: Size 6-12 treble, double or single
Tag: Flat or oval gold
Tail: Golden pheasant red breast feather
Rear body: Light or medium claret seal's fur
Rib: Oval gold tinsel
Middle hackle: Rich claret
Front body: Dark claret seal's fur
Rib: Fine oval gold tinsel
Front hackle: Two turns of hot orange cock or hen under two or three turns of badger
Eyes: Small jungle cock

A handsome pattern, incredibly successful for both fresh and resident fish in all conditions and seasons. Especially good on rainy days or in peaty water with flashes of sunshine. It works well in all sizes. Seal's fur (and not floss silk) is always used for the body. Jungle cock is mostly used for small eyes but larger jungle cock feathers can be used as wings. Rated highly, next to the Foxford Shrimp. A dressing by Robert McHaffie from the River Roe.

Claret Tail Bann Special Shrimp

PLATE 28

Hook: Size 6-12, treble, double or single
Tag: Flat or oval silver

Tail: Golden pheasant red breast feather dyed claret, wound
Rear body: Yellow floss
Rib: Oval silver
Middle hackle: Hot orange
Front body: Black floss
Rib: Oval silver
Wings: Roofed jungle cock
Front hackle: Badger
Head: Black

This is a another pattern not to be without on a spate river, or for jaded and back-end fish in the autumn. It is particularly good for sullen fish in low water. It works well in peaty water. Always use floss silk for the body.

This fly is one of the best shrimp flies tied low-water style. It is often fished in slow pools by casting upstream and across and then stripped slowly back. It once took twelve fish for an angler in an afternoon.

Collie Dog

PLATE 28

Body: A 3/4-inch plastic or aluminium tube
Hackle: A pinch of red hackle fibres or red bucktail at throat
Wing: Long black goat hair (2-4 inches long)

This is a really good pattern, especially in streamy water. It has taken more river spring salmon for me than any other fly and it can be equally good for summer grilse even in low water and bright sunshine. I have seen it take fish where both spinner and worm have failed. It will also take fish in a lough - in the stream where the river runs in.

The body materials can vary according to the fishing conditions. In heavy water in spring I use a 1-inch brass tube wrapped with embossed silver tinsel. In summer, I sometimes use a 3/4-inch plastic tube. In low water in either spring or summer I like a slim wing of either kid goat hair or a bunch of hair from the point of a fox squirrells tail, dyed black. The finer hair is more mobile in the low water. Otherwise the black goat hair is fine.

Connemara Black

PLATE 28

Hook: Size 6-10, single
Tag: Round fine silver tinsel and orange floss
Tail: Golden pheasant topping and Indian crow substitute
Rib: Oval silver tinsel
Body: Black seal's fur
Hackle: Black cock
Throat: Blue jay
Wing: Tippet in strands under bronze mallard

When a dark fly is called for it is hard to beat this well-proven, sombre-looking dressing. It is often used on the loughs for spring salmon. It makes an excellent dropper fly in small sizes (10 single), especially as a spate runs off.

Curry's Gold Shrimp

PLATE 28

Hook: Size 6-12, treble, double or single
Tag: Oval silver tinsel
Tail: Golden pheasant yellow breast feather, wound
Rear body: Embossed silver tinsel
Rib: Oval silver tinsel
Middle hackle: Hot orange
Front body: Embossed silver tinsel
Rib: Oval silver tinsel
Wings: Roofed jungle cock
Front hackle: Orange or golden olive
Head: Red

This is a dressing devised by Pat Curry of Coleraine. The original had orange toucan veilings at the sides. It is a good fly for fresh fish in bright weather and in coloured water. It is widely used on the Ballina Club waters of the Moy in coloured water in September.

Curry's Red Shrimp

PLATE 28

Hook: Size 6-12, treble, double or single
Tag: Oval or flat silver tinsel
Tail: Golden pheasant red breast feather, wound
Rear body: Red floss or seal's fur
Rib: Medium or Fine oval silver
Veilings: Red Swan strip or hackle points
Middle hackle: White-tipped badger
Front body: Black floss or seal's fur
Rib: Fine oval tinsel
Veilings: Red swan strip or hackle points
Wings: Jungle cock
Front hackle: White-tipped badger
Head: Red

This is the original shrimp fly, tied by Pat Curry of Coleraine, from which all the other shrimp patterns evolved. The original veilings were of Indian crow and tied at the sides.

It is still a very popular pattern and one will be found in nearly every salmon fisher's fly box in the country. It is especially good for fresh fish, is good in all types of light and water conditions and is a noted and successful lough salmon fly.

Delphi Badger

PLATE 29

Tying silk: Red
Body: Plastic tube, 1/2 inch
Dressing: An untidy bunch of badger hair tied all round
Head: Red

PLATE 27: SALMON FLIES

Top Row Beltra Badger, Botham's Fancy
1st Row Blue Charm
2nd Row Black Goldfinch, Black Doctor
3rd Row Ballynahinch Badger
Bottom Row Bann Special Shrimp, Ballina Grey Shrimp

The badger tube was the single most successful spring fish fly on the Bundorragha River for Seamus Henaghan, the Delphi gillie. It is interesting that the same dressing was used with equal success on Lough Fern in Donegal in its heyday as a spring salmon lough. Takes to a badger tube are usually savage and dramatic. It can be unbeatable on its day and an angler on the Owenea River in Donegal is reported to have risen 51 fish to it on one day.

It is also very good for grilse in small sizes on slow pools where the surface is well broken with a good ripple. In this situation if it is drawn across the pool, just under the surface - it must not skate - with the water bulging over the top of it, it will be chased and taken, especially by fresh grilse.

Drowes Dawn Tube Fly

PLATE 29

Tube: Size 3/4 - 3 inches
Tag: Flat gold tinsel
Rib: Oval gold tinsel
Body: Rear half, claret floss silk (Pearsalls); front half, yellow floss silk
Wing: Two bunches of dark red bucktail and two bunches of dark red bucktail tied in alternating bunches round the tube. The dark red colour is achieved by dying brown bucktail red (hair taken from the centre of the tail) and the resultant shade is closer to claret than red
Cheeks: Jungle cock over the dark red hair

This is a dressing from Hugh O'Connor from Garvary, Co. Fermanagh. It looks good when tied *and* in the water, and Hugh once hooked a fish on it on 1 January, opening day on the Drowes. It has earned its place in my box too and I especially like it for the Slaney.

Dusty Miller

PLATE 29

Hook: Size 4-10
Tag: Fine oval silver and yellow floss
Tail: Golden pheasant topping and Indian crow substitute
Butt: Black ostrich herl
Rear two-thirds, embossed silver tinsel; remainder, orange floss
Rib: Oval silver tinsel
Hackle: Golden olive over orange floss
Throat: Speckled guinea-fowl
Wing: Yellow, red and orange, bustard and golden pheasant tail, barred summer duck, narrow strips of bronze mallard, topping over all
Cheeks: Jungle cock

Sidney Spencer fished the loughs of the west and north-west of Ireland for salmon for thirty years. This was one of his favourite salmon flies, especially on days with a bit of light in the sky. It is still fished to the present day.

Dunkeld (Variant)

PLATE 29

Hook: Size 4-10, single or double
Tag: Oval gold and orange floss
Tail: Crest
Butt: Black seal's fur
Body: Flat gold tinsel
Hackle: Hot orange with blue jay or guinea-fowl dyed blue in front
Wing: Dyed brown squirrel or bucktail
Cheeks (optional): Blue hackle points

This is a dressing from the Moy and is very highly regarded in all seasons and in both coloured and clear water. A strip wing version tied with a body hackle and a pearl crystal hair underwing works well for spring salmon on Carrowmore Lake in Co. Mayo.

PLATE 28: SALMON FLIES

Top Row Connemara Black, Canadian Green, Claret & Jay
Middle Row Claret Shrimp, Collie Dog, Claret Tail Bann Special Shrimp
Bottom Row Curry's Gold Shrimp, Curry's Red Shrimp

Easky Gold Shrimp

PLATE 29

Hook: Size 6-12, treble, double or single
Tag: Flat or oval gold
Tail: Golden pheasant red breast feather, wound
Rear body: Oval gold tinsel in touching turns
Middle hackle: Hot orange
Front body: Oval gold tinsel in touching turns
Front hackle: Dyed red or scarlet
Eyes: Small jungle cock
Head: Black

This is a particularly successful fly on the Easky River in Co. Sligo, where it is used to great effect by Mr Frank Luce to take both salmon and seatrout. It is a cracking fly for the spate rivers, good in dark water, and seems to hold a particular attraction for big seatrout.

Erriff Nondescript

PLATE 29

Hook: Size 6-10, single or double
Tag: Fine round silver tinsel
Rib: Oval silver tinsel
Tail: Golden pheasant topping
Body: Black floss silk
Hackle: Badger cock
Wing: Red bucktail under badger hair

As the name indicates, this is an Erriff pattern. Its origin is unknown but it has proved to be quite effective when fished in low water in the streams on the lower beats.

Faughan Shrimp

PLATE 30

Hook: Size 6-12 treble, double or single
Tag: Oval gold tinsel

Tail: Golden pheasant red breast feather
Rear body: Orange floss
Rib: Medium or fine oval gold tinsel
Middle hackle: Burnt orange or dark orange (rich amber)
Front body: Dark claret floss
Rib: Fine oval gold tinsel
Wings: Jungle cock
Front hackle: Rich claret
Head: Black

This fly is used by several River Moy anglers to the exclusion of all others especially on the Swinford Club water. It probably works best on a dull day and can be fished in all water conditions. It is highly regarded as a spring salmon fly, even on the lough, and is particularly good on spate rivers. Floss silk is always used for the body material and the correct shade of the middle hackle is important. It is a dark or burnt orange and not hot orange.

Faughan Shrimp (Light)

PLATE 30

Hook: Size 4-12 single double or treble
Tag: Oval silver tinsel
Tail: Golden pheasant breast feather
Rear body: Golden olive/dirty yellow seal's fur
Rib: Oval or fine flat silver
Top veiling: Short tippet strands
Middle hackle: Short brown or red brown cock
Front body: Black seal's fur
Rib: Oval or fine flat silver
Top veiling: Tippet strands
Front hackle: Longish blue under long badger hackle
Head: Black

This is a popular back-end fly in Northern Ireland and is used with great success on the River Roe. It is also used on the Foyle system. This is a lovely fly and looks very good in the water.

Fiery Brown

PLATE 30

Hook: Size 4-10
Tag: Fine oval silver and yellow floss
Tail: A topping and tippets
Rib: Oval silver tinsel
Body: First quarter, orange seal's fur, second quarter, light blue seal's fur remainder, fiery brown seal's fur
Hackle: Fiery brown
Throat: Blue jay
Wing: Tippet in strands; married strands of red, blue, yellow and orange swan, bustard, golden pheasant tail; married teal and barred summer duck, brown mallard over
Head: Black

The Fiery Brown is still used today by a few anglers, especially in the south-west. It incorporates many of the traditional characteristics of Irish fly dressing, such as sparkling cock hackles and the sheen of natural seal's fur dyed in a variety of colours. It is sometimes considered to be an autumn fly but is just as likely to take a fish in the spring. No two flytying manuals give exactly the same dressing and I have adopted the above from Pryce-Tannatt and I don't think Michael Rogan, who probably invented it, would disagree with it.

Flashing Charmer

PLATE 30

Hook: 6-10, single or double
Tag: Fine oval silver tinsel and yellow floss
Rib: Oval silver tinsel
Tail: Golden pheasant topping
Body: Black floss
Hackle: Kingfisher blue cock
Wing: Grey squirrel tail with five or six strands of pearl Lurex over the top

This is a flashing version of the hairwing dressing of the Blue Charm. It was first popularised in this country at Burrishoole, by Viscount Mills, where it proved very effective on Lough Feeagh when fished on the point early in the season. It can score well in any of the Connemara fisheries when fished in small sizes.

Fluorescent Green Shrimp

PLATE 30

Hook: Size 6-12 treble, double or single
Tag: Oval gold
Tail: Golden pheasant red breast feather, wound
Rear body: Fluorescent green floss
Rib: Oval gold
Middle hackle: Creamy badger
Front body: Fluorescent green floss
Rib: Oval gold
Wing: Jungle cock, roofed
Front hackle: Creamy badger
Head: Red

This is a brilliant August-September fly in a small dirty flood. It will take resident fish in heavily coloured water and on its day will outfish almost any other fly. Strangely, it is not recommended for use earlier in the season.

Foxford Shrimp

PLATE 30

Hook: Size 6-12 treble, double or single
Tag: Oval silver tinsel
Tail: Golden pheasant red breast feather
Rear body: Black seal's fur
Rib: Oval or fine flat silver
Middle hackle: Badger (white-tipped)
Front body: Fiery brown seal's fur
Rib: Oval or fine flat silver
Wing: Jungle cock roofed, or eyes on smaller sizes

Front hackle: Rich ginger
Head: Red

Anglers who like to fish shrimp flies regard this as one of the best. It is a great all-round fly and unbeatable for jaded fish from July onwards. It is equally good for fresh fish on spate rivers, for fish in low, clear water and in heavily coloured water late in the season. It will often not only interest fish, but take good numbers of fish when nothing else will work. This is a brilliant fly with a history of successful exploits too numerous to mention here.

The fiery brown seal's fur for the body should have a reddish tinge and the front ginger hackle colour is important, being a rich gleaming ginger shade - almost cinnamon in colour - often found on a farmyard cockerel. Some anglers prefer to use a dark chocolate brown or a furnace hackle as the front hackle.

This is an exact copy of a fly used by an old angler (now deceased) from the Midlands with devastating effect on the Moy at Foxford. No one caught more fish than he did. He used only two fly patterns, the Foxford Shrimp and the Goat.

The successes attributable to the Foxford Shrimp are legion. One true story will suffice. A group of tourists were watching an angler on the Ballina Club water during an August spate. He caught several good fish before hooking a much larger fish. The angler played it for some time but the fish slipped free of the hook just as it approached the net. While this was of great concern to the tourists it did not seem to bother the angler unduly. He went on fishing and was soon into a small fish which, with a quick and unexpected dart, took him round a rock and broke the line. The angler became extremely upset, throwing down his rod. 'Whats the matter? Sure, that was just a small fish compared to the one before,' said one of the tourists consolingly. 'It's not the

fish,' said the angler, 'it's the fly. He's away with my last Foxford Shrimp.'

Foxton Badger

PLATE 00

Tube: Brass, aluminium or plastic, $1/2$ - 2 inches
Rib: Flat silver tinsel followed by oval silver tinsel
Body: Black floss
Wing: Well marked white-tipped badger hair with a long-fibred kingfisher blue hackle doubled and tied in at the head

This is a dressing used very successfully by Tom Foxton, a fisherman on the Slaney.

It has all the ingredients of a good fly and I am not surprised that there are anglers who will not fish the Slaney in April without it. It is at its best when the water is clear. It is also used at Castleconnell and on west of Ireland rivers.

Fox & Orange

PLATE 30

Hook: Size 6-10, single or double
Rib: Flat silver tinsel
Tail: Golden pheasant topping
Body: Black floss silk
Hackle: Hot orange cock
Wing: Hair from a foxs brush
Cheeks: Jungle cock

This is one of Dr Francis Briggs' flies for the Erriff. It is a simple fly, with no frills, but with a lot of action in the water. I like it especially when a flood is falling.

Galway Black & Yellow

PLATE 31

Hook: Size 6-10 double or treble
Tag: Fine oval gold tinsel

PLATE 29: SALMON FLIES
Top Row Drowes Dawn Tube, Dusty Miller, Delphi Badger
Middle Row Erriff Nondescript, Dunkeld (Variant)
Bottom Row Easky Gold Shrimp

Tail: Golden pheasant topping
Rib: Fine oval gold tinsel
Body: Flat gold tinsel
Hackle: Lemon yellow cock
Wing: Black squirrel

A fly for the Galway Weir Fishery when the grilse are running. Always worth a try with this fly at dusk.

Galway Green

PLATE 31

Hook: Size 6-10, double or treble
Tag: Oval silver tinsel
Rib: Oval silver tinsel
Tail: Bunch of black squirrel tail
Body: Yellow floss silk
Hackle: Bunch of yellow bucktail tied in as a beard hackle
Wing: Bucktail dyed Green Highlander

I am sure you have learned by now that when an angler tells you he took a fish on a particular named pattern, the dressing may be far removed from what you expect. In fact he may be selling you a dummy. So, when someone tells you at the Galway Fishery that he took his fish on a Green Highlander, it is quite likely he means this pattern. It was introduced to the fishery by a Scotsman, Charlie Stevens. It is usually dressed on a size 10 treble and fished on a sink-tip line. I would not be happy going to the Galway Weir in May or June without this fly dressed on trebles in sizes 8, 10 and 12.

Garry Dog

PLATE 31

Hook: Size 4-12, single, double or treble
Tag: Fine round silver tinsel and yellow floss
Rib: Oval silver tinsel
Tail: Golden pheasant topping
Body: Black floss

Hackle: A bunch of dyed blue speckled guinea-fowl
Wing: Red bucktail under yellow bucktail

Here we have what I consider to be one of the most useful dressings of modern times for river fishing for salmon. It can be dressed on a single hook, a double, a treble or a tube - and all are equally effective. When dressing this pattern on a treble hook, I usually omit the tail and tie the wing long (at least twice the length of the hook shank).

Garry Dog Tube Fly

PLATE 31

Tube: 1/2-3 inches
Rib: Wide oval or flat silver tinsel
Body: Black floss silk
Wing: Two bunches of red and two bunches of yellow bucktail, tied in alternating bunches around the tube
Hackle: Dyed blue guinea fowl tied at the head
Head: Black

The Garry Dog tube is a great all round fly and particularly effective in coloured water. It can be tied on tubes up to 3 inches long of plastic, aluminium, brass or copper, depending on the depth at which it is required to swim. An important fly for both spring and autumn in heavy water.

General Practitioner

PLATE 31

Hook: Size 6-10, single, double or treble
Tying silk: Red or orange
Long whiskers: 5 or 6 fibres from a golden pheasant spear feather
Short whiskers: Golden pheasant red breast feathers
Prawn head: Tippet feather tied in between

two golden pheasant red breast feathers with the concave sides facing each other
Rib: Oval gold tinsel
Body: Orange seal's fur
Hackle: Orange cock palmered
Back feathers: Tippets and golden pheasant red breast feather
Head: Red varnish

The General Practitioner, or GP as it is more usually called, was invented by Colonel Esmond Drury in the 1950s. It is probably the best imitation of a shrimp or prawn ever invented. It can be deadly fished in small sizes on a floating line in low water. Some prefer to fish a big fly on a sunk line raising and lowering the rod tip.

The tying procedure is a little complicated and the number of back feathers varies with the size of the hook. It was on a GP that I took my first Scottish salmon on a size 6 single at Dalreoch on the River Stinchar.

Ghost Shrimp

PLATE 31

Hook: Size 6-12 single, double, treble
Tag: Oval or flat silver
Tail: Golden pheasant breast feather, wound
Rear body: Yellow floss
Rib: Oval silver
Veilings: Orange hackle points
Middle hackle: White
Front body: Black floss
Rib: Oval or flat silver
Veilings: Orange hackle points
Wings: Roofed jungle cock
Front hackle: White tipped badger
Head: Black

This is a really good fly for a bright day. It is a cracking fly for fresh grilse in either bright or dull weather and it is excellent in coloured water.

Goat

PLATE 31

Hook: Size 6-10 single, double or treble
Tag: Oval silver
Tail: Topping
Butt: One turn of black seal's fur
Body: Light grey seal's fur
Rib: Oval silver over grey fur only
Hackle: Yellow
Wing: Yellow kid goat or squirrel hair

A fly by the same unknown angler on the Moy who gave us the Foxford Shrimp. It is an old pattern now, even though it is a hairwing. It is good at most times for both fresh and resident fish and is very effective in peaty water and sunlit conditions. Regarded by many to be better than the Lemon & Grey. One of the nice things about this fly is that it is easily seen in the water and therefore you can watch it and see the fish take.

Gold Bug

PLATE 31

Hook: Size 6-12 treble, double or single
Tag: Flat or oval gold
Tail: Golden pheasant breast feather, wound
Rear body: Oval gold tinsel in touching turns
Middle hackle: Hot orange
Front body: Oval gold tinsel in touching turns
Wings: Jungle cock or one teal breast feather
Front hackle: Red game or light brown
Head: Black

The Gold Bug is an excellent fly in heavily-coloured water at any time in the season. The wing may be roofed jungle cock or single-eyed teal breast feather, tied on top as a veiling.

Goshawk Hairwing

PLATE 31

Hook: Size 6-10, single, double or treble
Tag: Oval gold
Tail: Yellow topping feather with red hackle point fibres or swan strip over but tied shorter than the topping feather
Body: Black seal's fur or floss silk
Rib: Oval or fine flat gold or silver. Usually gold
Hackle: Rich claret with optional blue jay or dyed blue guinea-fowl at throat
Wing: Rich yellow bucktail
Head: Black

This is an old river Moy fly and is still popular and effective both there and elsewhere. It is good all season and in any water, coloured or clear. It is especially noted for taking difficult fish. On larger versions, a body hackle of the same colour as the throat hackle may be used.

Other variations are the Blue Goshawk, the Orange Goshawk, and the Black Goshawk, which have blue, orange and black hackles respectively.

Goshawk (Variant)

PLATE 32

Hook: Size 6-10 single or double
Tag: Oval silver and yellow floss
Rib: Oval silver tinsel
Tail: Slip of red goose or swan
Body: Black floss
Hackle: Blue jay at throat
Wing: Married slips of yellow, red and yellow swan

I first dressed this pattern on the advice of Geoff Hearns, the gillie on the Ridge Pool on the Moy. Contrary to popular belief that the fishing on the Ridge Pool is ridiculously easy, it can be quite the opposite, even when there are lots of fish there. This is a great fly in medium water dressed on a size 12 Partridge low-water double (Code Q1). It once took seven grilse for a friend of mine on an otherwise difficult day and it has saved the day for me at the Ridge Pool on more than one occasion.

Green Butt

PLATE 32

Hook: Size 6-10 single or double
Tag: Fine oval silver tinsel and DFM green floss
Rib: Oval silver tinsel
Tail: Golden pheasant topping
Body: Black floss
Hackle: Black cock
Wing: Black squirrel tail

This North American salmon fly is quite popular in the west of Ireland, especially on the Connemara fisheries. It is fished in summer and the fluorescent green tag appears to give it an added attraction or arouse the aggression in fish that have been resident in a pool for some time. Also useful as a dropper on Lough Beltra.

Green Highlander

PLATE 32

Hook: Size 4-10 single or double
Tag: Fine oval tinsel
Tail: Golden pheasant topping
Butt: Black ostrich herl
Body: Rear quarter, yellow floss; front three-quarters, green floss
Rib: Oval silver
Hackle: Green cock over the green floss
Throat: Yellow cock
Wing: Tippet in strands, married orange, yellow and green swan, peacock wing, peacock sword and brown mallard and topping over all

124

PLATE 30: SALMON FLIES

Top Row Faughan Shrimp, Faughan Shrimp (Light)
1st Row Fiery Brown
2nd Row Flashing Charmer, Fox & Orange
Bottom Row Flourescent Green Shrimp, Foxford Shrimp

The old record books of the Galway Fishery make frequent references to this pattern, highlighting its effectiveness on that particular fishery. The phenomenon of certain patterns becoming associated with certain fisheries is, I believe, more than chance. I think it has to do with the shades and colours in the surrounding environment and how certain flies blend in with and complement the environment in which they are fished. The Green Highlander and the Galway Fishery is a case in point. The tone of this nicely matches the green of the bottom vegetation and the cream limestone rock of the river bed.

Green Highlander (hairwing)

PLATE 32

Hook: Size 6-10 single or double
Tag: Flat silver
Tail: Golden pheasant topping
Body: Black floss
Rib: Oval silver and fluorescent green floss
Hackle: Yellow
Wing: One part yellow under, one part orange under, two parts Green Highlander kid goat or dyed green squirrel, tied long
Head: Black

This is an Albert Atkins variant and regarded by many as the single most successful fly for fresh fish in bright weather. Robert Gillespie says that nothing comes close to it in glaring, sunny weather. It is best in clear water and very good on the Galway Weir. It is not recommended for resident fish.

Grey-Winged Salmon Gosling

PLATE 32

Hook: Size 8-10 bronzed double
Tying silk: Black

Rib: Wide oval gold tinsel
Tail: Fibres of cock pheasant centre tail
Body: Golden olive seal's fur
Hackle: Hot orange cock, long in fibre, doubled and tied sloping well back
Wing: Grey mallard flank tied in as a hackle (doubled and sloping back)

This is a very good spring salmon fly and good for fresh grilse too in either bright or dull weather. There is great life, glow and movement in it if it is tied correctly and it is very good on a rainy day on the Moy. It is an excellent lough fly too, especially on Lough Melvin and Lough Conn.

Hairy Mary

PLATE 32

Hook: Size 4-10, single or double
Tag: Fine oval gold tinsel
Rib: Oval gold tinsel
Tail: Golden pheasant topping
Body: Black floss
Hackle: Kingfisher blue cock
Wing: Brown bucktail or natural red squirrel

This is another of the great salmon flies and one that I am never without. It is probably at its best from May to September and I often put it on in a smaller size if I rise a fish to another fly and get a refusal. It can be an excellent dropper fly on the river when fished in small sizes.

Halpin

PLATE 32

Hook: Size 6 or 8, single or double
Tag: Fine oval silver
Tail: Golden pheasant topping
Butt: Red wool
Rib: Oval silver
Body: Black floss silk
Hackle: Dyed red cock

Throat: Pale blue dun
Wing: Grey squirrel with a topping over
Head: Red varnish

This is a dressing from the River Feale in north Kerry, a river that gets a good run of spring salmon and a big run of autumn fish after the nets come off. The Halpin is regarded as being a really excellent late-season fly, and one can see why. Local anglers believe that the red colours in the dressing trigger aggression in the cock fish.

Howard's Claret Shrimp

PLATE 32

Hook: Size 6-12, treble, double or single
Tag: Oval gold with optional butt of red seal's fur
Tail: Golden pheasant red breast feather dyed claret, wound
Body: Rich dark claret seal's fur
Rib: Medium or wide flat gold tinsel
Wings: Jungle cock (large)
Hackle: A bunch of claret or scarlet hair tied on top and bottom
Head: Black

This is another great fly from the River Roe, first tied by Howard Reilly. It is extremely popular on the Moy. It is a great autumn fly and spate-river fly and is particularly good in peaty water. The large jungle cock wings make it easy to see in dark water, a feature that should inspire confidence in the angler. It is also good in clear water on a dull day.

Irish General Practitioner (GP)

PLATE 33

Hook: Size 8-12, trebles, doubles or singles
Tag: Flat or oval gold
Tail: Golden pheasant red breast feather, wound, with a short V-shaped tippet feather as a top veiling
Rear body: Orange seal's fur
Rear hackle: Hot orange, palmered
Rib: Medium or fine oval gold tinsel
Veiling: A short tippet feather or strands, on top only
Front body: Hot orange seal's fur
Front hackle: A smaller hot orange hackle, palmered
Rib: Fine oval gold tinsel
Veiling: A small golden pheasant red breast feather laid on top (not wound)
Head: Red or black

The Irish GP, a River Mourne pattern, uses the standard shrimp fly tail of golden pheasant red breast feather. Many anglers consider the Irish version to be a more effective fly than the original. It is mainly used in the smaller sizes (10s and 12s, doubles or trebles). The hot orange dressing given above is used only for very fresh fish and in coloured water. The more popular tyings are more muted, using bodies and hackles of fiery brown, claret or golden olive. These shades seem to be more effective for older fish in clear water.

Sometimes two golden pheasant red breast feathers of different sizes are used for the veiling of the front body in order to give a layered shell-back effect. On smaller sizes the body may be made as one piece and not jointed.

Jeannie

PLATE 33

Hook: Size 6-8, single or double
Tag: Oval silver tinsel
Rib: Oval silver tinsel
Tail: Golden pheasant topping
Body: Rear third, pale yellow floss; front two-thirds, black floss
Hackle: Natural black cock
Wing: Brown bucktail or red squirrel

I have only observed the hairwing version of the Jeannie used in this country. It is an old Scottish Dee pattern, dressed in the original with a bronze mallard wing. The hairwing version (above) is quite successful for summer salmon in clear water.

Jock Scott

PLATE 33

Hook: Size 4-10, single or double
Tag: Fine oval silver tinsel
Tail: A topping and Indian crow substitute
Butt: Black ostrich herl
Rib: Oval silver tinsel
Body: Rear half, yellow floss; front half, black floss
Hackle: Black cock over black floss
Throat: Speckled guinea-fowl
Wing: Strips of white-tipped turkey tail, married slips of peacock wing, yellow, red and blue swan, bustard, golden pheasant tail, two strands of peacock sword; married strips of teal and barred summer duck, bronze mallard over and a topping over all
Cheeks: Jungle cock

How could I leave out this beautiful fly? It is probably the most complicated of all to tie, with up to fifty different pieces in the fully dressed version. It is not widely used nowadays, though it is still stocked by some of the fisheries which like to maintain things old, good and traditional, such as Newport House and Delphi Lodge in Co. Mayo. Few who can doubt its effectiveness in the past and Dr Ken Whelan, the Director of the Salmon Research Agency at Burrishoole, told me that when he examined the records from 1925-83 for the Erriff he found that it was among the top three most effective flies for thirty-two seasons out of fifty-eight. Nowadays, I tie the above abridged version which I think still retains all the essential features of the original.

Jock Scott Shrimp

PLATE 33

Hook: Size 6-12 single, double or treble
Tag: Flat or oval silver
Tail: Golden pheasant red breast feather, wound
Rear body: Light yellow floss
Rib: Medium oval silver
Veiling: Red swan strips or hackle points
Middle hackle: Badger cock hackle
Front body: Black floss
Rib: Fine flat silver
Veiling: Red swan strips or hackle points
Wings: Roofed jungle cock
Front hackle: Badger
Head: Red

This is a very close relative of Curry's Red Shrimp, the only difference being that the rear body is yellow instead of red. This is an excellent pattern and many think that it surpasses the Curry's Red in peaty water and spate rivers.

John Anthony Shrimp

PLATE 33

Hook: Size 6-12, single, double or treble
Tag: Oval gold
Tail: Golden pheasant red breast feather, wound
Rear body: Black floss silk
Rib: Oval gold tinsel
Middle hackle: Medium red game
Front body: Black floss or fur
Rib: Fine oval gold
Wings (optional): Jungle cock
Front hackle: Medium red game
Head: Black

The late John Anthony O'Donnell, a postman from the Glenties, Co. Donegal, was probably the single most successful angler on the Owenea River. This was his

PLATE 31: SALMON FLIES

Top Row Galway Black & Yellow, Garry Dog Tube, Galway Green
Middle Row General Practitioner, Garry Dog, Goat
Bottom Row Gold Bug, Goshawk Hairwing, Ghost Shrimp

favourite fly, said to be made from materials he found in his wife's sewing basket and with hackles from a farmyard rooster. It was good enough for him and good enough too for the thousands of fish he landed in his lifetime from the Owenea River.

This fly is still used on the Moy with great success, often in difficult conditions, by those brave enough to give it a try, for it looks very ordinary. The jungle cock wing is optional, as the original fly did not have it.

In his latter years John Anthony had the fly tied for him by the late Laurence Cunningham of Drumaho, Derry, and the rear half of the body was dressed with embossed gold or silver tinsel and a tail of purple-dyed golden pheasant breast feather.

Juner Shrimp
(Chris Downey)

PLATE 33

Hook: Size 6-12, treble, double or single
Tag: Oval or flat gold
Tail: Golden pheasant red breast feather, wound
Rear body: Red seal's fur or floss
Rib: Oval or fine flat gold
Middle hackle: Yellow
Front body: Purple seal's fur or floss
Rib: Oval or fine flat gold
Front hackle: Purple
Head: Black

The Juner is a pattern devised by Chris Downey, the manager of the Foxford Fishery's private beats on the Moy. It is an excellent fly for fresh fish in June, hence its name, and it is noted for taking fish in cold weather or when there is a cold north wind on the water. It sometimes pays to move it fast through the water.

Kenyaman

PLATE 33

Hook: Size 6-10 single
Tail: Golden pheasant topping
Body: Wide oval silver tinsel
Wing: Yellow goat or squirrel hair
Hackle: Black hen, long in fibre, tied full circle

This fly has its origins at the Burrishoole Fishery in Co. Mayo, obviously brought there by an angler from Kenya in the 1950s. It always brings back fond memories to me because it was on a variant I caught my first salmon at the Corrigeens on Lough Furnace. The battle went on for nearly an hour. The late Tom Chambers was boatman and Rev. George Miller from Cavan my boat partner.

Kenyaman (Variant)
(Peter O'Reilly)

PLATE 33

Hook: Size 8 Mustad 7948A
Rib: Oval silver tinsel
Tail: Slip of orange swan
Body: Flat silver tinsel
Hackle: Black cock, long in fibre

Lemon & Grey

PLATE 34

Hook: Size 4-10, single or double
Tag: Fine oval silver and yellow floss
Tail: Golden pheasant topping and Indian crow substitute
Butt: Black ostrich herl
Rib: Oval silver tinsel
Body: Light grey seal's fur
Hackle: Grizzle cock
Throat: Lemon cock
Wing: Tippet in strands, married green, yellow and orange swan, bustard, peacock

130

wing and golden pheasant tail; teal and summer duck; bronze mallard
Head: Black

The Lemon & Grey is not exactly the first fly a newcomer to salmon fishing would pick from a fly box. With its muted shades of grizzle and grey on the body, it is not very attractive to the eye. However, it appears to be seen in an entirely different light by the salmon and, in my opinion is equally good, when fished in different sizes, as both a spring fly and a summer fly.

It is probably at its best when fished in water that has a bit of colour or dark stain in it. For this reason it fishes well on the dropper in spring on Lough Beltra, and a friend, to whom I gave a couple of size 8 singles, once did great damage on the Cork Blackwater in July.

Lemon & Grey Hairwing

PLATE 34

Hook: Size 6-10, single or double
Tag: Flat silver
Tail: Golden pheasant topping
Butt: One turn of black seal's fur
Body: Light grey seal's fur
Rib: Oval silver tinsel
Body hackle (optional, for larger sizes only): Grizzle
Throat hackle: Yellow
Wing: One part of orange under; two parts of brown squirrel tail
Head: Black

This is a west of Ireland hairwing version of the classic Lemon & Grey. It converts very well to a hairwing pattern and is a favourite on the Moy for spring fish and fresh grilse. It can also be good for taking a fish when times are hard. But it helps if the weather is dull.

Lemon Shrimp

see Yellow Shrimp

Logie

PLATE 34

Hook: Size 4-10 single
Tying silk: Primrose
Tag: Fine round silver tinsel
Rib: Oval silver tinsel
Tail: Golden pheasant topping
Body: Rear third, lemon yellow floss; front two-thirds, red floss
Hackle: Kingfisher blue cock
Wing: Slips of swan or goose dyed yellow and veiled with bronze mallard

This Scottish fly is popular on the River Moy. The dressing favoured has the traditional feather wing rather than the modern hairwing version. It can be especially effective for grilse in summer when dressed on a size 10 single hook.

McDermott's Badger

PLATE 35

Hook: Size 4-10 double, single or small tube
Tying silk: Black
Tag: Oval silver
Rib: Oval silver tinsel
Tail: Golden pheasant topping
Body: Flat silver tinsel
Hackle: Yellow
Wing: Badger hair
Cheeks: Jungle cock
Head: Black

This is a pattern attributed to the late Dr Piggins of Burrishoole and tied and used by Pat McDermott, the gillie on the Newport River. It is a beautiful, yet simple dressing and catches a lot of spring fish.

PLATE 32: SALMON FLIES

Top Row Goshawk (Variant), Green Butt
1st Row Grey-Winged Salmon Gosling
2nd Row Green Highlander, Green Highlander (hairwing)
3rd Row Howard's Claret Shrimp
Bottom Row Halpin, Hairy Mary

PLATE 33: SALMON FLIES
Top Row Irish General Practitioner, Jock Scott Shrimp
1st Row Jock Scott
2nd Row John Anthony Shrimp, Juner Shrimp
3rd Row Jeannie
Bottom Row Kenyaman, Kenyaman Variant

Magenta Shrimp

PLATE 34

Hook: Size 6-12, treble, double or single
Tag: Flat or oval silver
Tail: Golden pheasant red breast feather
Rear body: Red seal's fur
Rib: Oval or fine flat silver
Middle hackle: Light magenta
Front body: Black seal's fur
Rib: Oval silver
Wings/Eyes: Jungle cock
Front hackle: Badger
Head: Black

There are few flies to better this one for bright-weather grilse fishing. An angler once took nineteen grilse from one pool on it on a bright windy day. A really good bright-weather, fresh-fish fly.

Mar Lodge

PLATE 35

Hook: Size 6-12
Tag: Fine round silver tinsel
Tail: Golden pheasant topping and a small jungle cock feather
Butt: Black ostrich herl
Rib: Oval silver tinsel
Body: Flat silver tinsel jointed in the middle with a couple of turns of black floss
Hackle: Speckled guinea-fowl
Wing: Tippet in strands; married strands of white swan, bustard, cinnamon, grey matted and brown matted turkey tail, summer duck; topping over all
Cheeks: Jungle cock

It is always amazes me how popular this pattern still is today. Its origin, as the name suggests, is on the River Dee in Scotland, but it is still fished in Ireland in its fully dressed form for spring fish. A reduced version of it, tied on a bronze trout hook -

size 10 and 12 - is considered an excellent brown trout and seatrout fly and is widely fished in Kerry, especially on loughs Leane and Currane.

Michael Angelo

PLATE 35

Hook: Size 6-10, single, double or treble
Tag: Fine round silver tinsel and yellow floss
Rib: Oval silver tinsel
Tail: A slip of red swan or goose
Body: Black floss silk
Hackle: A bunch of dyed blue guinea-fowl tied in at the throat
Wing: Yellow bucktail under red bucktail

This fly has its origin in Limerick. It is closely related to the Garry Dog. It is popular on the Shannon at Plassey and on the Mulcair River when fresh fish are running and the water is clearing after a flood.

Mourne Claret Shrimp

PLATE 34

Hook: Size 4-12, single, double or treble
Tag: Flat or oval gold
Tail: Golden pheasant breast feather
Rear body: Very dark claret seal's fur
Rib: Oval gold tinsel
Middle hackle: Very dark claret
Front body: Black seal's fur
Rib: Oval or fine flat silver
Front hackle: Badger
Eyes: Small jungle cock
Head: Black

The colours in this fly are very subdued and it is really a pattern for clear water. It is not as widely used as the Claret Shrimp.

Mourne Orange & Gold Shrimp

PLATE 34

Hook: Size 6-12, treble, double or single
Tag: Flat or oval gold tinsel
Tail: Golden pheasant red breast feather
Rear body: Orange seal's fur
Rib: Oval gold tinsel
Middle hackle: Hot orange
Front body: Black seal's fur
Rib: Fine flat silver tinsel
Front hackle: Badger
Eyes: Small jungle cock
Head: Black

Another truly great fly from the River Mourne which many consider to be as good as, if not better than, the standard Orange & Gold Shrimp. A great fly for either fresh or jaded fish in any water conditions. A roofed jungle cock wing may be used instead of the eyes (see above).

Mourne Purple & Gold Shrimp

PLATE 34

Hook: Size 6-12 treble, double or single
Tag: Flat or oval gold
Tail: Golden pheasant breast feather wound
Rear body: Purple seal's fur, medium
Rib: Oval gold
Middle hackle: Purple
Front body: Black seal's fur
Rib: Fine flat silver
Front hackle: Badger
Eyes: Small jungle cock
Head: Black

This is regarded as a great fly for late-running fish. Using the correct shade of purple for both body and hackle results in a beautiful fly that shows up well in the water.

The shade of purple must not be too dark.

Mourne Red Shrimp

PLATE 34

Hook: Size 4-12, single, double or treble
Tag: Flat or oval gold
Tail: Golden pheasant breast feather wound
Rear body: Very dark red seal's fur
Rib: Oval gold or fine flat gold
Middle hackle: Very dark red
Front body: Black seal's fur
Rib: Oval or fine flat silver
Front hackle: Badger
Eyes/Wings: Small jungle cock or roofed jungle cock
Head: Black

This is a great killing pattern on the River Mourne and preferred by the anglers there to the bright reds and scarlets used in other red shrimp patterns. The red seal's fur and middle hackle used in this fly are very dark red, almost a ruby-wine colour. A really beautiful and effective fly.

Moy Green (Chris Downey)

PLATE 35

Hook: Size 6-10 single, double or treble
Tag: Oval silver
Rib: Oval silver
Tail: Golden pheasant topping
Body: Flat silver
Throat hackle: Hot orange tied as a beard hackle only
Wing: Grey squirrel dyed Green Highlander
Head: Black

This is a Chris Downey fly for the Moy and it works well for fresh fish in either clear or coloured water. It is an exceptionally good dropper fly for fresh grilse and works very well in bright weather and in the evening in calm, still conditions after a hot day.

Moy Green Peter

PLATE 35

Hook: Size 8-10 bronze double
Tying silk: Black
Rib: Fine flat silver
Body: Pale olive seal's fur
Wings: Strips of hen pheasant centre tail or speckled oak turkey tied long on top and under the hook. The top wing is slightly longer
Hackle: One light red game or ginger cock tied as a collar

This is a favourite pattern for the Swinford Water on the Moy in July, August and September. It works best in dull weather and clear water and takes not only fresh fish, but jaded fish as well.

Munro Killer (Dark)

PLATE 35

Hook: Size 4-10, single, double or treble
Tag: Oval gold tinsel
Rib: Oval gold tinsel
Tail: Golden pheasant topping
Body: Black floss
Throat hackle: Hot orange cock, wound or tied as a beard hackle under fibres of blue jay or dyed blue speckled guinea-fowl
Wing: One part yellow squirrel, and one part orange squirrel under two parts black squirrel

This is one of the modern Scottish hairwing dressings which is widely used in Ireland. I am equally happy fishing it dressed on a single, double or treble hook. I like it on a falling spate on west of Ireland rivers and it is a deadly fly for grilse on the Galway Fishery when dressed on a size 10 or 12 Esmond Drury treble. Try it anywhere in the evening as the light fades on calm water or fast smooth glides. One of the best.

Munro Killer (Light)

PLATE 35

Hook: Size 6-10, single, double or treble
Tag: Oval or flat gold
Tail: Orange hackle point
Body: Black floss
Rib: Fine flat gold
Hackle: Hot orange wound with a few blue guinea-fowl fibres at the throat
Wing: Barred grey squirrel tail dyed yellow
Head: Black

This is regarded as a great fly for spring fish and for fresh grilse. It is good in all conditions, but particularly so in peaty spate rivers, when the water is coloured.

Nephin Shrimp

PLATE 36

Hook: Size 6-12, single, double or treble
Tag: Fine oval silver
Tail: Golden pheasant red breast feather
Body: Black floss
Rib: Wide oval silver tinsel
Wing: One jungle cock feather on top
Hackle: Dark orange
Head: Black

This is a fly for the north Mayo rivers and Lake Carrowmore. It is probably at its best in coloured water on a bright day. On the larger patterns two jungle cock feathers are tied as a roof wing. A single feather tied flat is used on sizes 10 and 12.

Octopus Shrimp

PLATE 36

Hook: Size 6-12 treble, double or single
Tag: Oval silver or flat silver
Tail: Golden pheasant red breast feather
Rear body: Yellow floss
Rib: Oval silver tinsel

PLATE 34: SALMON FLIES

Top Row Lemon & Grey, Lemon & Grey (hairwing), Logie
1st Row Mourne Red Shrimp, Mourne Purple & Gold Shrimp
2nd Row Mourne Orange & Gold Shrimp
Bottom Row Mourne Claret Shrimp, Magenta Shrimp

Middle hackle: White; then over this several strands of crystal hair veiling, tied all round, but sparse
Front body: Black floss or seal's fur
Rib: Oval silver tinsel
Front hackle: Red game or light brown
Head: Black or red

This pattern was first tied by a Frenchman, Jean-Luc Martin, for the Moy. It is good in both coloured and clear water and while better for fresh fish, it nevertheless takes its share of resident spring fish as well. It is especially popular because it does not require jungle cock. It once accounted for seventeen fish over two days for one angler on the Ridge Pool during a small dirty late-summer spate when no one else caught anything.

Orange & Gold Shrimp

PLATE 36

Hook: Size 6-12, treble, double or single
Tag: Flat or fine oval gold or silver
Tail: Golden pheasant red breast feather
Rear body: Medium or wide oval gold tinsel in touching turns
Middle hackle: Hot orange
Front body: Black seal's fur
Rib: Oval gold tinsel
Front hackle: Badger
Head: Black

For the Orange & Copper fly, replace the gold tinsel with copper tinsel.

The Orange & Gold Shrimp is regarded as a fantastic spate-river fly where its heavier, slim body makes it ideal for fast flows and it glows in the peaty water. A good all-round fly for both fresh and jaded fish. It is an especially useful modern fly in that the dressing does not call for the use of jungle cock.

Owenea Shrimp

PLATE 36

Hook: Size 6-12 single, double or treble
Tag (no tail required): Flat or oval gold
Rear body: Flat gold tinsel
Rib: Fine oval gold
Middle hackle: Golden pheasant yellow rump feather either natural or dyed orange
Front body: Black seal's fur
Rib: Fine oval or flat silver tinsel
Wings: Jungle cock
Front hackle: Badger
Head: Red

This is another fly for the Owenea River and It is also used successfully in other rivers of the north and west. The dressing is as given by Robert McHaffie in *Trout and Salmon*.

Purple & Gold Shrimp

PLATE 36

Hook: Size 6-12, single, double or treble
Tag: Flat or oval gold
Tail: Golden pheasant red breast feather, wound
Rear body: Oval gold tinsel, touching turns
Middle hackle: Purple
Front body: Oval gold tinsel, touching turns
Front hackle: Badger
Head: Black

This is a late-season fly and will take difficult fish in poor fishing conditions.

There is a Donegal version of this pattern using a red floss front body and a red head. It is used by Russell Whiteman, from Derry, and is much better for fresh grilse and just as effective for the difficult ones.

Purple Bug

Hook: Size 6-12, treble, double or single
Tag: Flat or oval gold

Tail: Golden pheasant breast feather, wound
Rear body: Oval gold tinsel in touching turns
Middle hackle: Purple
Front body: Oval gold tinsel in touching turns
Wing: Teal breast feather
Front hackle: Furnace or brown
Head: Black

The Purple Bug is a late-summer and back-end fly for clear water.

The wing may be either roofed jungle cock or a single eyed teal breast feather tied on top as a veiling. Larger Bugs often have strands of hair or hackle points tied as veilings above and below. Calf tail hair is popular because of its crinkle. They may be the same colour as the middle hackle or a complementary colour, such as red or hot orange. Strips of swan are used as veilings on the smaller flies.

Quack

PLATE 36

Hook: Size 4-8 single
Tag: Fine round silver tinsel and yellow floss
Tail: Golden pheasant topping
Butt: Red wool
Rib: Oval silver tinsel
Body: Black floss silk
Wing: Tippet in strands, red blue and yellow swan, slips of bronze mallard and a topping over all
Head: Red varnish

Whoever named this fly (and I suspect it was the late Owen Mullins of Newport House) had a sense of humour for, as the name suggests, it is closely related to the Black Doctor. It is used for spring salmon on Lough Beltra and the Newport River and is said to be a good evening pattern.

Red & Gold Shrimp

PLATE 36

Hook: Size 6-12, treble, double or single
Tag: Oval gold
Tail: Golden pheasant breast feather, wound
Body: Oval gold tinsel in touching turns
Veiling: Red swan strips above and below
Front hackle 1: Scarlet or dark red
Wings: Split jungle cock
Front hackle 2: Badger
Head: Red

This is a variation on the Red Shrimp theme, the difference being that it has a shorter, one-piece body. A truly excellent autumn fly. Those who use it claim that late-running grilse and Autumn fish cannot resist it. It is at its best on a dull day and is equally good in clear or coloured water.

Shrimp Fly

PLATE 37

Hook: Size 6-12 treble, double or single
Tag: Flat or oval silver
Tail: Golden pheasant breast feather, wound
Rear body: Red floss
Rib: Oval silver
Middle hackle: Hot orange
Front body: Black floss
Rib: Oval silver
Front hackle: Badger
Wings: Roofed jungle cock or small jungle cock eyes
Head: Red

This pattern is referred to by tyers as simply 'The Shrimp Fly', with no qualifying name. Confusingly, many anglers losely refer to every shrimp pattern as a shrimp fly. Nevertheless this is a very specific pattern and it is an excellent all-round fly, especially for difficult fish in August and for use in dark peaty water.

Silver Badger

PLATE 37

Hook: Size 6, 8, 10, single or double
Tag: Fine round silver and yellow floss
Tail: Golden pheasant topping
Butt: Black ostrich
Rib: Oval silver tinsel
Body: Flat silver tinsel
Hackle: Kingfisher blue cock
Wing: Badger hair

This is the silver-bodied version of the Badger. It is popular in Mayo and Connemara and is very effective for fresh grilse in low water when dressed on a size 10 double hook.

Silver Doctor

PLATE 37

Hook: Size 4-10, single and size 10 and 12 double
Tag: Fine oval silver tinsel and yellow floss
Tail: Golden pheasant topping and kingfisher-blue hackle point
Butt: Red wool
Rib: Oval silver tinsel
Body: Flat silver tinsel
Hackle: Pale kingfisher or Cambridge blue cock with widgeon in front at the throat
Wing: Tippet in strands; married red, blue and yellow swan, bustard, peacock wing and light mottled turkey; narrow strips of teal or summer duck; bronze mallard over and a topping over all
Head: Red varnish

This is one of my favourite salmon flies for both fresh spring fish and later fresh grilse in June and July. Fish it on a sunk line or sink-tip in spring and on a floating line in summer. I always use the feather-wing dressing and would never consider the hairwing version. I find this fly extraordinarily effective for fresh grilse when fished on its own in small sizes (size 10 double). Here I use an abbreviated version of which retains all the essentials of the original fully dressed fly - topping for a tail, red butt, silver body, blue throat hackle, mallard wing, topping, and red head.

Silver Erriff

PLATE 37

Hook: Size 6-10 single or double
Tag: Flat gold tinsel
Tail: Golden pheasant topping
Butt: Black ostrich herl
Rib: Oval silver tinsel
Body: Flat silver tinsel
Hackle: Kingfisher blue cock
Wing: Badger hair with golden pheasant topping over

This is a perky little fly that easily falls into the Badger category of flies. The golden pheasant topping over the wing and the flat gold tag give it an extra bit of flash and make it an ideal fly for either fresh spring fish or fresh grilse on the river that gives it its name. It probably takes more fish when fished in smaller sizes (size 8 and 10 single or size 10 double) and I have no doubt that it will take a fish on any west of Ireland river or anywhere where the water runs clear without peat stain.

Silver Grey

PLATE 37

Hook: Size 4-10 single
Tag: Fine oval silver tinsel and golden yellow floss
Tail: Golden pheasant topping
Butt: Black ostrich herl
Body: Flat silver tinsel
Hackle: Badger cock from the second turn

PLATE 35: SALMON FLIES
Top Row Munro Killer (Dark), Munro Killer (Light)
1st Row Mar Lodge
2nd Row Moy Green, McDermott's Badger
3rd Row Michael Angelo
Bottom Row Moy Green Peter

of tinsel

Throat: Teal or widgeon
Wing: Tippet in strands; married strands of white, yellow and green swan, bustard, peacock wing, golden pheasant tail; strips of teal or barred summer duck; bronze mallard and topping over all
Cheeks: Jungle cock

This pattern first came to my attention many years ago on Lough Beltra, as a good fly for spring salmon. I have also used it on the rivers further south in Connemara and one can see why because it is an unusually attractive and really beautiful fly yet it lacks a lot of the colour associated with traditional built-wing flies. It is usually fished on the dropper on the lough and can be effective even in a small ripple when there is a touch of mildness in the air. I would also fish it on the river on a bright day after the water has cleared.

Silver Rat

PLATE 37

Hook: Size 4-10, single or double
Tying silk: Red
Tag: Oval gold tinsel
Rib: Oval gold tinsel
Tail: Golden pheasant topping
Body: Flat silver
Wing: Silver fox or grey squirrel tail
Hackle: Grizzle cock, doubled and tied full circle in front of the wing
Head: Red varnish

I was first shown a chewed up version of this fly on the Erriff in 1982. The angler who owned it did not know its name and a full year passed before I discovered that it was a Silver Rat.

That angler's praise for it and confidence in it impressed me so much that I made a note of the dressing. I am glad I did, for it has saved the day for me on a number of important occasions. It has caught fish everywhere from the Drowes to Castleconnell on the Shannon.

I like it especially in low clear water dressed on size 12 and 14 Partridge Low Water Wilson doubles (code 02).

Silver Shrimp

PLATE 37

Hook: Size 6-12 treble, double or single
Tag: Oval or flat silver
Tail: Golden pheasant red breast feather, wound
Rear body: Flat silver tinsel or embossed silver or medium-to-wide oval silver tinsel in touching turns
Rib: Fine oval silver (used on flat tinsel bodies only)
Veilings: Hot orange hackle points above and below
Middle hackle: White-tipped badger
Front hackle: Flat silver tinsel or embossed silver tinsel in touching turns
Veilings: Hot orange hackle points above and below
Front hackle: Badger
Head: Black or red

This is a dressing from the Mulcair River and the Shannon. It is an excellent fly for fresh fish and is very good in bright conditions and has scored well in coloured water. It is regarded as a fly mainly for extreme conditions.

Silver Stoat's Tail

PLATE 37

Hook: 6-12, single or double
Tag: Fine oval silver tinsel
Rib: Oval silver tinsel
Tail: Golden pheasant topping
Body: Flat silver tinsel
Hackle: Black cock

Wing: Stoat's tail or black squirrel tail

There are many who consider this fly to be closely related to the Stoat's Tail.

There the story ends. It is a good fly by day and not long ago an angler took five fish on it in one morning at Ballynahinch. But I think it is at its best when fished in the fading light, last thing before dark. It is equally good for fresh grilse in June or late-running fish at the end of the season.

Silver Wilkinson

PLATE 37

Hook: Size 4-10, single or double
Tag: Oval silver tinsel & golden yellow floss
Tail: Golden pheasant topping and Indian crow substitute
Butt: Red wool
Rib: Oval silver tinsel
Body: Flat silver tinsel
Hackle: Magenta cock with widgeon in front
Wing: Tippet in strands; married strands of red, blue and yellow swan, peacock wing, bustard and light mottled turkey tail; teal; bronze mallard over; a topping over all
Head: Black varnish

Here is a salmon fly that has stood the test of time. It is very close in the dressing to the Silver Doctor, yet there are anglers who will ask for it by name. I tend to think of it as an early-season fly for spring fish and a size 6 dressing is probably the most effective when there is a nice push of clear water going through the pool. It is a fly to try over a fish that has failed to respond to a Silver Doctor or one of the other flashy flies. Fish it slowly in the stream and then handline it in short darts as it comes into the slack water.

Stoat's Tail

PLATE 38

Hook: Size 6-12 single or double
Tag: Oval silver tinsel
Rib: Oval silver tinsel
Tail: Golden pheasant topping
Body: Black floss silk
Hackle: Black cock
Wing: Stoat's tail or black squirrel tail

I sometimes think that the Stoat's Tail is not far removed from the Black Pennell. It is a first-class salmon fly on the river and always worth a try in clear water both for fresh fish and grilse, right through to September.

Taylor Special

PLATE 38

Hook: Size 6-12, single or double
Tying silk: Black
Tag: Oval silver tinsel
Tail (optional): Three or four strands of peacock sword fibres
Rib: Oval silver tinsel over front half only
Body: Rear half, fluorescent green floss; front half, peacock herl
Veiling: A strand of fluorescent green floss over the rear half only
Wing: Grey squirrel tail dyed green
Hackle: Yellow cock, tied as a collar

This dressing is by the American angler-artist Arthur Taylor from Maine. It does well on this side of the Atlantic too and is especially good for fresh fish. It is not often that someone is embarrassed by the success of a fly but that is exactly what happened to me one morning on the Ridge Pool on the Moy. I hooked fish after fish on it while the other four rods struggled. In the end I took it off and gave it to one of the others and he promptly took a fish. I like it best tied on small doubles (10s and 12s) for the grilse.

Thunder & Lightning

PLATE 38

Hook: Size 4-10, single or double
Tag: Fine round silver tinsel and orange floss (some tyers use yellow floss)
Tail: Golden pheasant topping
Butt: Black ostrich
Rib: Oval gold tinsel
Body: Black floss
Hackle: Orange from the second turn of the rib (from the rear)
Throat: Blue jay or dyed blue guinea-fowl
Wing: Bronze mallard (topping optional)
Cheeks: Jungle cock

This has to be one of the most popular of Irish salmon flies. I have seen it used from the Slaney in the south-east to the Moy and Lough Beltra in the north-west and it will always take a fish. I like it best when it is lightly dressed and fished at dusk in small sizes - even down to a size 10 single. A really good fly for spring fish on either lough or river and equally good for grilse.

Thunder & Lightning Tube

PLATE 38

Tube: From 3/4 to 2 inches
Rib: Oval or embossed gold tinsel
Body: Black floss
Wing: Pale orange bucktail tied on top and under only
Hackle: Blue jay, sparse
Cheeks: Jungle cock

A tube fly dressing by Kevin Clayton for the Lee in Cork. It is very effective there and no doubt it would work well on other waters.

Thunder Stoat

PLATE 38

Hook: Size 6-12, single, double or treble

Tag (optional): Oval gold
Tail: Yellow hackle fibres over red hackle fibres
Body: Black floss
Rib: Oval gold
Hackle: Hot orange with blue jay, or guinea-fowl dyed blue, over at the throat
Wing: Black bucktail or black squirrel hair
Cheeks: Jungle cock
Head: Black

There are many versions of this fly but this is one of the best - a really exceptional fly. It is consistent, reliable and dependable and there is no situation where this fly will not take fish. It even looks good in the water.

An alternative version of the Thunder Stoat which works well in many parts of Ireland in small sizes (10 and 12 doubles), especially as a dropper fly, is:

Tag: Gold wire
Rib: Gold wire or very fine oval gold tinsel in close turns but not touching
Body: Black tying silk, varnished
Hackle: Hot orange beard hackle
Wing: One part yellow-dyed grey squirrel tail under one part orange-dyed grey squirrel tail under two parts black squirrel tail

Tippet Badger Shrimp

PLATE 38

Hook: Size 6-12, treble, double or single
Tag: Oval gold
Tail: Golden pheasant red breast feather, wound
Rear body: Golden olive or rich yellow seal's fur
Rib: Oval gold
Middle hackle: Short tippet strands at top under creamy badger
Front body: Purple seal's fur
Rib: Oval gold
Front hackle: Short tippet strands at top under creamy badger

PLATE 36: SALMON FLIES

Top Row Nephin Shrimp, Octopus Shrimp
1st Row Orange & Gold Shrimp, Owenea Shrimp
2nd Row Quack
Bottom Row Purple & Gold Shrimp, Red & Gold Shrimp

Head: Black or red

Those who use this fly soon become devotees and would not be happy to be without it. It is a brilliant fly for late season and peaty water. Particularly useful in an autumn flood on a spate river. A wonderful fly for jaded fish.

Tosh

PLATE 38

Hook: Size 6-12 double or single
Tag: Fine oval silver tinsel
Rib: Oval silver tinsel
Body: Black floss silk
Hackle: A pinch of yellow bucktail
Wing: Black squirrel

The Tosh was first brought to my attention by Jim Stafford, the manager of the Erriff Fishery. He noted that it was effective on various types of water, from the fast-running lower beats right up to the slower pools at the top of the river. I consider it is at its best in summer and autumn in clear water when dressed lightly and fished in small sizes (10 or 12 doubles). I fish it on the dropper on a two-fly cast. It took my first Boyne salmon at Blackcastle one September morning and friends to whom I gave it praise its effectiveness highly on that river.

Vambeck

PLATE 39

Hook: Size 6-12 single or double
Tying silk: Black
Tag: Fine oval silver tinsel
Rib: Fine oval silver tinsel
Tail: Golden pheasant crest
Body: Flat silver tinsel
Hackle: Black cock doubled and wound at the head only
Wing: Dyed black squirrel tail

Eyes: Jungle cock

This is a dressing by Louis Vambeck of Mullingar. He gave it to me with a good recommendation and I have to say it has proved its worth, especially late in the evening and for autumn fish. It is now one of my favourite patterns and once took three fish when the other five rods on a beat blanked. It also took my best ever salmon. I prefer it tied on standard double hooks in sizes 8, 10 and 12. I think it is important that the hackle be doubled before winding.

White Shrimp

PLATE 39

Hook: Size 6-12, single, double or treble
Tag: Flat silver
Tail: Golden pheasant red breast feather
Rear body: Flat silver
Rib: Fine oval silver
Middle hackle: White or light cream cock or hen
Front body: Flat silver
Rib: Fine oval silver
Front hackle: Strips of grey mallard all round
Head: Black

This is an unlikely-looking but deadly salmon fly which can work well in all seasons and conditions. Perhaps it is because it looks different that it is so deadly. Fish are unlikely to have seen anything like it before. It has often succeeded when other flies have failed and it is always as well to have one in the box. It is fatally attractive to fresh grilse and its advocates claim that even if there is only one fresh fish in a pool it can be taken out with a White Shrimp. Try it on a summer evening or on wild a overcast day. Best in sizes 8 and 10.

Many anglers prefer to take the middle hackle from a hen cape.

Wilkinson Shrimp (dark)

PLATE 39

Hook: Size 4-10, single, double or treble
Tag: Oval or flat silver
Tail: Golden pheasant red breast feather
Rear body: Flat silver tinsel, embossed silver tinsel, or medium-to-wide oval silver tinsel in touching turns
Rib: Fine oval silver (used on flat or embossed tinsel bodies only)
Middle hackle: Rich kingfisher blue
Front body: As rear body
Wings (optional): Roofed jungle cock
Front hackle: Dark claret
Head: Black

The Dark Wilkinson Shrimp is a fly for bright weather and clear water only. It is very popular on the Moy, where it has a great reputation for taking fish - even resident spring fish - on glaring bright days.

The Light Wilkinson Shrimp has a magenta middle hackle and Cambridge blue front hackle, jungle cock wings and a red head.

The Light Wilkinson Shrimp is the most popular pattern. It is widely used and works well for fresh fish especially in bright weather when there is just a little colour in the water. It is a good spring salmon fly and is very popular on the Delphi Fishery, Lough Beltra and on the Newport River.

Willie Gunn

PLATE 39

Hook: It can be dressed on single, double or treble hooks or on tubes from 1/2 inch to 3 inches long
Rib: Oval gold tinsel
Body: Black floss
Wing: Yellow bucktail, under orange bucktail, under black bucktail

This is one of the modern range of hairwing salmon flies that has found its way to Ireland. It is used fairly frequently on west coast fisheries and its great strength is its versatility both in terms of size and dressing. It can be dressed on single, double or longshank treble hooks, tubes or Waddington shanks. The shade of the fly can be altered to suit the colour of the water by adding or reducing the amount of the various colours of hair in the wing. For example, add more yellow hair and you have a brighter fly for coloured water. This is a great fly that can be fished from the beginning to end of the season.

The wing on small sizes (10 and 12 doubles) can be tied with squirrel hair, and this version can be very effective in summer.

Yellow Dolly (Derek Knowles)

PLATE 40

Hook: Size 16 or 18, treble
Body: Thin red tube 1/4 to 5/8 inch long
Hackle: The second half of the dressing is a skirt of stiff yellow deerhair and the front half is stiff black hair, both tied all round and trimmed neatly
Head: Red varnish

Derek Knowles's Yellow Dolly is an exceedingly successful salmon dry fly and has taken fish for the inventor on several north of England rivers, in Scotland and in Connemara. I know an angler who fishes it with great success on the upper reaches of the Cork Blackwater. Derek's favourite time for fishing it is when a spate has run off and the conventional fly is only stirring the occasional fish. My friend on the Cork Blackwater concurs with this, but claims it will also take resident fish if cast repeatedly over them. Always worth a try in a good ripple or a small wave on deep, slow pools.

PLATE 37: SALMON FLIES
Top Row Silver Badger, Silver Doctor, Silver Erriff
1st Row Shrimp Fly
2nd Row Silver Grey, Silver Rat
3rd Row Silver Shrimp
Bottom Row Silver Wilkinson, Silver Stoat's Tail

PLATE 38: SALMON FLIES

Top Row Stoat's Tail, Taylor Special, Thunder & Lightning
1st Row Thunder & Lightning Tube, Foxton Badger
2nd Row Tosh, Thunder Stoat
Bottom Row Tippet Badger Shrimp

Yellow Shrimp (or Lemon Shrimp)

PLATE 40

Hook: Size 6-12 treble, double or single
Tag: Oval silver tinsel
Tail: Golden pheasant red breast feather
Rear body: Yellow seal's fur or floss
Rib: Oval silver tinsel
Middle hackle: Rich yellow or light yellow
Front body: Black seal's fur or floss
Rib: Oval silver tinsel
Front hackle: Badger
Eyes: Small jungle cock
Head: Black

The Yellow Shrimp is a good early and late season fly, especially when the water is dark and peaty. It is a good catcher of spring fish on the Moy. The shade of the hackle and body can vary from lemon yellow through all the shades of yellow to golden olive. However, in order to create a good-looking fly it is important to keep the colour of the hackle and body the same. Many people like to tie this fly with a red head.

Wings of larger jungle cock feathers sometimes replace the eyes.

Yellow & Silver Shrimp

PLATE 40

Hook: Size 6-12 treble, double or single
Tag: Oval or flat silver
Tail: Golden pheasant red breast feather wound
Rear body: Oval silver tinsel in touching turns
Middle hackle: Yellow
Front body: Black seal's fur or floss
Rib: Oval or fine flat silver
Front hackle: Badger
Head: Black or red

This is a fly that many anglers would not want to be without on the Moy. It takes a lot of spring fish and is good for coloured water or bright weather.

Yer Man

PLATE 40

Hook: Size 2-6 Partridge double for spring fishing; 8-14 double for summer/autumn
Tail: Mixture of red, orange, brown bucktail
Ribs: Oval gold tinsel and monofilament
Eyes: Monofilament (20-30lb) burnt and tied in with figure-of-eight turns and a touch of Superglue to hold it in place
Body: Mixed red and claret seal's fur
Hackle: Dark red dyed cock
Shell back: Slip of 500 gauge clear polythene cut to shape and tied in with the monofilament
Head: Black

Yer Man was originally devised by Peter Wolstenholme and Michael Brown for the Bandon River. Their preference was to fish the fly for salmon, but they were somewhat disappointed with their lack of success compared with anglers who fished the natural shrimp. And so they set about producing a fly that would attract more fish. By all accounts they succeeded and I can hear 'What did you get that one on,' and the reply 'Yer Man,' ring out along the Bandon Valley. They emphasise the importance of sparkling cock hackles and natural seal's fur when tying their fly. It can be tied with lead wire under the shank for spring fishing.

MINI-TUBES

Mini-Tubes have become very popular, especially for summer fishing, in recent years. They can be fished on floating, sink-tip or intermediate lines, according to water conditions, and are excellent takers of both resident and fresh fish in all conditions.

They are especially good in low water as the buoyancy offered by the tube means that they can be fished very slowly and made to hang over the fish without sinking. These flies remain close to the surface even when they stop moving and this can be very attractive to the fish.

Because the tubes are so light, they have a tendency to skate in fast water and this has to be guarded against. The tube should fish just under the surface, with the water humping over it. This is especially attractive to fresh fish and to seatrout at night. The Exe Tube is noted for taking big seatrout, as well as being a good salmon fly.

Mini-Tubes are very good hookers of fish. A size 14 treble is used and, while it usually takes a very good hold, fish should not be played too severely.

Half-inch plastic tubes are used and the length of the finished fly - head to end of wing - is one inch. Tags, bodies and wings should be varnished with clear varnish before and after tying to prevent the tinsel slipping or unravelling.

Some Mini-Tubes are dressed as standard tube flies, with the wing tied all round. Others are tied as if hooks were being used, with a wing on top and beard hackle of hair or hackle fibres. For example, the Willie Gunn is tied all round while the Goshawk is dressed with a wing and throat hackle.

Badger

PLATE 23

Tube: 1/2 inch
Tag: Fine flat or oval silver tinsel
Rib: Fine flat or oval silver tinsel
Body: Black floss
Wing: Badger hair
Throat: Blue hackle fibres
Head: Black

Badger & Orange

PLATE 23

Tube: 1/2 inch
Tag: As badger above
Rib: As badger above
Body: Black floss
Wing: Orange hackle fibres
Head: Black

The Badger Shrimps are: Badger & Orange, Badger & Red, Badger & Golden Olive.

Black & Orange

PLATE 23

Tube: 1/2 inch
Tag: Fine flat or oval silver tinsel
Rib: Fine flat or oval silver tinsel
Body: Black floss
Wing: Orange and black bucktail tied in quarters
   The orange bucktail is tied in first and slightly more black than orange is used

Black & Yellow

As Black & Orange, but with yellow hair replacing the orange.

Black Dart

PLATE 23

Hook: 1/2 inch
Tag: Six turns of fine oval gold or copper tinsel
Rib: Fine oval gold or copper tinsel
Body: Black floss silk
Wing: Hot orange bucktail tied on top of and under the body
Cheeks: Jungle cock
Head: Black

Dunkeld

PLATE 23

Tube: 1/2 inch
Tag: Fine oval gold tinsel
Rib: Fine oval gold tinsel
Body: Flat gold tinsel
Wing: Orange and blue bucktail tied all round with brown bucktail on top only
Head: Black

Exe Tube

PLATE 23

Tube: 1/2 inch
Tag: Fine oval silver tinsel
Rib: Fine oval silver tinsel
Body: Flat silver tinsel
Wing: Orange-dyed grey squirrel tail tied all round
Head: Black

A wing of red-dyed grey squirrel tail makes the Exe Tube into a Towy Tube.

Garry Dog

PLATE 23

Tube: 1/2 inch
Tag: Fine flat or oval silver tinsel
Rib: Fine oval silver tinsel
Body: Black floss
Wing: Red bucktail under yellow bucktail tied on top and under
Cheeks: Blue bucktail or squirrel tied at the sides and shorter than the wing

Goshawk

PLATE 23

Tube: 1/2 inch
Tag: Fine oval or flat gold tinsel
Rib: Fine oval or flat gold tinsel
Body: Black floss

Wing: Rich yellow dyed bucktail on top only
Throat: Claret hackle fibres under blue-dyed guinea-fowl hackle fibres

Green Highlander

PLATE 23

Tube: 1/2 inch
Tag: Fine flat or oval silver tinsel
Rib: Fine flat or oval silver tinsel
Body: Black floss
Wing: One part yellow bucktail, under one part orange bucktail, under two parts Green Highlander-dyed bucktail, tied all round
Head: Black

Moy Green

PLATE 24

Tube: 1/2 inch
Tag: Fine oval silver tinsel
Rib: Fine oval silver tinsel
Body: Flat silver tinsel
Wing: Green-dyed grey squirrel tail on top only
Throat: Hot orange hackle fibres
Head: Black

Munro Killer (dark)

PLATE 24

Tube: 1/2 inch
Tag: Fine flat or oval gold tinsel
Rib: Fine oval gold tinsel
Body: Black floss
Wing: One part yellow bucktail under one part orange bucktail under two parts black bucktail
Throat: Orange hackle fibres with blue-dyed guinea-fowl (sparse) in front
Head: Black

PLATE 39: SALMON FLIES
Top Row Vambeek, White Shrimp
1st Row Wilkinson Shrimp (Light)
2nd Row Willie Gunn, Wilkinson Shrimp (Dark)
Bottom Row Willie Gunn (Waddington)

Munro Killer (light)

PLATE 24

Tube: $1/2$ inch
Tag: Fine flat or oval gold tinsel
Rib: Fine oval gold tinsel
Body: Black floss
Wing: Yellow-dyed grey squirrel tail on top only
Throat: Orange hackle fibres with blue-dyed guinea-fowl (sparse) in front
Head: Black

Shrimp Fly

PLATE 24

Tube: $1/2$ inch
Tag: Six turns of fine oval silver or gold tinsel
Rib: Fine oval silver or gold tinsel
Body: Red floss
Wing: White bucktail (sparse) under orange bucktail tied on top of and under the tube
Cheeks: Jungle cock
Head: Red

Silver Badger

PLATE 24

Tube: $1/2$ inch
Tag: Fine flat or oval silver tinsel
Rib: Fine oval silver tinsel
Body: Flat silver tinsel
Wing: Badger hair
Throat: Blue hackle fibres
Head: Black

Silver Stoat

PLATE 24

Tube: $1/2$ inch
Tag: Fine oval or flat silver tinsel
Rib: Fine oval silver tinsel

Body: Flat silver tinsel
Wing: Black squirrel tail tied all round
Head: Black

Stoat's Tail

PLATE 24

Tube: $1/2$ inch
Tag: Fine flat or oval silver
Rib: Fine oval silver
Body: Black floss
Wing: Black squirrel tail tied all round
Head: Black

Thunder & Lightning

PLATE 24

Tube: $1/2$ inch
Tag: Fine flat or oval gold tinsel
Rib: Fine oval gold tinsel
Body: Black floss
Wing: Yellow, red and orange bucktail (sparse) under dyed brown bucktail tied on top of and under the tube
Cheeks: Short fibres of dyed-blue guinea-fowl at the sides
Head: Black

Towy Tube

see Exe Tube (page 152)

Wilkinson

PLATE 24

Tube: $1/2$ inch
Tag: Fine flat or oval silver tinsel
Rib: Fine oval silver tinsel
Body: Flat silver tinsel
Wing: Natural brown bucktail on top only
Throat: Magenta-dyed hackle fibres with blue-dyed hackle fibres (sparse) over
Head: Red

Willie Gunn

PLATE 24

Tube: 1/2 inch
Tag: Fine flat or oval gold tinsel
Rib: Fine oval gold tinsel
Body: Black floss
Wing: One-third yellow and one-third orange bucktail tied all round under one-third black bucktail - sometimes a little extra black bucktail is used
Head: Black

PLATE 40: SALMON FLIES

Top Row Yellow Shrimp
Middle Row Yellow & Silver Shrimp
Bottom Row Yellow Dolly, Yer Man

Index

Bibliography

Bates, J.D. *The Art of the Atlantic Salmon Fly* 1987

Clarke, B. *The Pursuit of Stillwater Trout* 1975

Clegg, T. *The Truth About Fluorescents* 1967

Cove, A. *My Way with Trout* 1986

Edwards, O. *Oliver Edwards' Flytyers Masterclass* 1994

Elder, F. *The Book of the Hackle* 1979

Fallon, N. *Fly Fishing for Irish Trout* 1983

Falkus, H. *Salmon Fishing* 1984

Gathercole, P. *The Handbook of Flyting* 1989

Goddard, J. *Trout Fly Recognition* 1966

Goddard, J. *Stillwater Trout Flies* 1969

Goddard, J. *Stillwater Flies, How and When to Fish Them* 1982

Goddard, J. *Waterside Guide* 1988

Harris, J.R. *An Anglers Entomology* 1952

Ivens, T.C. *Still Water Fly Fishing* 1952

Jorgensen, P. *Salmon Flies, Their Character and Style* 1978

Kennedy, M. *Trout Flies for Irish Waters*

Kingsmill Moore, T.C. *A Man May Fish* 1983

Murray and Ryan *Trout Flies*

Lapsley, P. *The Complete Fly Fisher* 1990

Malone, E.J. *Irish Trout and Salmon Flies* 1984

Martin, D. *Fly Tying Methods* 1987

Pryce-Tennatt, T.E. *How to Dress Salmon Flies* 1977

Roberts, J. *River Trout Flies* 1989

Robson, R. *Robson's Guide* 1985

Sawyer, F. *Nymphs and the Trout* 1958

Skues, G.E.M. *The Way of a Trout with a Fly* 1949

Skues, G.E.M. *Minor Tactics of the Chalk Stream* 1924

Veniard, J. *Fly Dresser's Guide* 1952

Veniard, J. *Further Guide to Fly Dressing* 1964

Waddington, R. *Waddington on Salmon Fishing* 1991

Wakefield, J. *Flytying Techniques* 1980

Walker, C.F. *Lake Flies and their Imitation* 1969

Weaver, M. *The Pursuit of Wild Trout* 1991

Whelan, K. *The Angler in Ireland* 1989

Wilson, D. *Fishing the Dry Fly* 1987